WHEN
REASON FAILS

Psychotherapy
in America

WHEN
REASON FAILS

*Psychotherapy
in America*

ROBERT A. LISTON

Macrae Smith Company

PHILADELPHIA

Copyright © 1972 by Robert A. Liston

Library of Congress Catalog Card Number 72– 4381
Manufactured in the United States of America
Published simultaneously in Canada by
George J. McLeod, Limited, Toronto

ISBN 0–8255–5313–X

Book design by Anne Churchman

7209

To Felicia

. . . whose name is herself

Contents

Introduction

Some years ago the English language was enriched by the expression "like a rat in a maze." It suggests a person who is feeling or acting lost, confused and a bit trapped. The expression was borrowed from a famous psychological experiment in which the psychologist releases a rat into a maze of blind alleys and circuitous passageways. The rat runs around aimlessly, eventually finding the route that leads to food at its end. The exercise is repeated, while the psychologist counts the number of trials and the length of time it takes the rat to learn to go unerringly to the food. The experiment is considered valuable in studying how animals, including people, learn.

In writing this book, I feel an awful lot like the rat. At least I have great sympathy for it, for the study of psychology truly resembles a maze. One can wander around for a very long time and seem to get nowhere.

Part of the problem with a book of this type is that

psychology is a very large study. By a common definition, psychology is a science that studies the behavior of
man and other animals. In so doing, the study of psychology laps over into biology, physics, chemistry and other
physical sciences, mathematics and statistics, medicine,
economics, philosophy, literature, history, sociology,
education—to name a few disciplines. A most aggrandiz-
ing science is psychology!

Even when they stick to their behavioral "knitting,"
psychologists are working on a very large piece of cloth.
They are particularly interested in such matters as
growth and development of children; motivation and
emotional behavior of people (which can help them understand, explain and predict what people do or might
do in given situations); perception, through which they
can discover how the five senses (seeing, hearing, smell-
ing, tasting and touching) function and how disorders of
perception develop; learning and thinking, to discover
how a person learns, thinks and remembers, as well as
how he might do them better; individuality and personality; conflict and mental health, in order to help people
to live more productive and satisfying lives; and social
behavior, in hopes of resolving some of the conflicts and
maladjustments of society. And that list merely men-
tions the high points. It is like describing the world's
mountain ranges by listing the six highest peaks.

Psychology is a major field of study and a highly popular one. A person can major in it in college, then attend
a university to earn his master's and doctoral degrees in
the subject, following which he may be expected to train
in a hospital or other institution before going to work.
No one studies psychology *per se*. He zeroes in on some
branch of the field, such as educational, industrial or

design psychology, psychological testing, clinical psychology, or child psychology.

So large is the subject of psychology that in almost any year more than 15,000 books are published in the field and most of them have the size and height to make excellent doorstops.

The path I have taken through this maze of material is the one labeled *psychotherapy*. This is a book about the various theories and methods that have been developed for treating mentally ill and/or emotionally and behaviorally disturbed people. This is one of the most popular fields of study in psychology and what most people think of when they refer to psychology. It is a subject not ordinarily taught to younger readers, but I believe it is one in which young people are intensely interested, for their own enlightenment and for introduction to a fascinating field as well. Certainly it is a subject everyone talks about, especially parents and teachers.

Even the small piece of psychology known as psychotherapy is too big for this book. The published works of Sigmund Freud, generally considered the father of modern psychotherapy, fill twenty-four volumes, and most of the other therapists described in this book were scarcely less prolific with the pen. In 1959, psychologist Robert A. Harper wrote a highly popular book, *Psychoanalysis and Psychotherapy*. It provides brief descriptions of 36 different systems of psychotherapy—and Harper left out several systems at the time. It is further estimated that another dozen or so major methods have been developed since. Indeed, it is not too much of an exaggeration to state that there are almost as many systems as there are people to advocate and practice them.

How can we wend our way through such a vast subject? Obviously, we must limit it. I have done this in several ways. Reluctantly, I have omitted the rather fascinating psychotherapeutic methods of the ancient Greeks and Romans, as well as the techniques used in medieval and Renaissance days. This book begins with Freud and proceeds toward the present. For practical purposes, it is a book about psychotherapy in this century.

I have made no effort to include *all* systems of psychotherapy. I have concentrated upon those major systems which are either widely practiced or have been of great influence upon later systems. For example, the "individual psychology" of Alfred Adler, the first of Freud's disciples to break away from the master, is not widely practiced in the United States today. But both his theory and his method have had a great influence on other systems that are practiced today.

The organization of the book is rather simple. Following an opening chapter describing psychotherapy and those who practice it, I have divided the book into two parts, treating first of those systems which seek to cure the patient by giving him insight into the underlying causes of his disturbance, and, second, of those systems which largely ignore insight and concentrate upon teaching the person to correct his behavior. Few experts will quarrel with this division, but some eyebrows may be raised about the amount of space given to the learning therapists. I am aware that most therapists practice some form of insight therapy. I have given greater space to the relatively smaller group of learning therapists because their work is interesting and considerably less has been written about it for the general public.

There are instant problems in writing a book on psychotherapy. In a short space it is impossible to describe a complete theory including all its uses and ramifications. I have tried to report briefly and as accurately as possible the major elements of the theory and the method of practicing it.

Another problem is controversy. Few subjects in America are as controversial as psychotherapy. I will have more to say about this in the first chapter, but at this point let it be known that I have tried to report each system as fairly and objectively as possible, while providing a variety of criticisms that have been made of it, so that the reader may be able to make up his own mind as to its wisdom and efficacy. Perhaps, too, the reader will be able to form some judgments about the whole role of psychotherapy in modern society.

Still another problem is terminology. Like scientists, doctors, sociologists, economists and other experts, psychologists have a love for the obtuse. It is a case of "why use an understandable word when a complex one of many syllables will do?" And how much better if it is derived from Latin or Greek! Whenever possible, I have tried to simplify the terminology. When it has not been possible, I have explained. In truth, the study of psychotherapy is not *that* difficult. Most of the concepts are relatively simple, and many fall into the category of common sense. Thus, you may be pleasantly surprised how much you know about the subject, even if you have never read a word about it.

I am indebted to more people than I can possibly remember. I should like to single out those people who made books available to me for my intensive research. At my alma mater, Hiram College, in Ohio, Miss Constance Jenkins, a senior student, and Miss Thelma Bumbaugh, the college librarian. In New York City, Mrs. Marjorie Newstrand, a dear friend and practicing psychologist. In

Washington, D. C., Mrs. Eleanor R. Seagraves, a librarian, who has a talent for knowing the type of material I need and sending it to me by the ton.

During nearly twenty years of writing as a newspaperman, magazine journalist and author, I have interviewed, collaborated with or otherwise learned from a large number of psychiatrists, psychologists and other experts on the human mind. I cannot identify them all, so I am restricting myself to three who have been particularly helpful. My friend Robert G. Amick, a psychologist on the faculty of Mt. San Antonio College in California, taught me much during many psychological "bull sessions." R. M. N. Crosby, M. D., is a Baltimore neurologist and neurosurgeon. We collaborated on a book, *The Waysiders* (Delacorte Press, 1968) during which I learned a great deal about brain function and the psychology of perception. Most especially I am indebted to Dr. Willard Mainord, professor of psychology at the University of Louisville. During a protracted collaboration on a book, I became interested in psychotherapy as a field of study and learned a great deal from him.

Robert A. Liston
Benalmadena Costa
Spain

WHEN
REASON FAILS

*Psychotherapy
in America*

1

Psychotherapy
Who, What and How

What is psychotherapy? A popular dictionary defines it as "the application of various forms of mental treatment, as hypnosis, suggestion, psychoanalysis, etc., to nervous and mental disorders." A leading college textbook says psychotherapy "embraces a wide variety of techniques whose goal is to help the emotionally disturbed individual modify his behavior so that he can make a more satisfactory adjustment to his environment."

A number of definitions could be cited, but all have a common characteristic. They are all extremely broad. They use such nonspecific terms as "various," "wide variety," "disorders," "disturbed individual," "satisfactory adjustment." The result is that psychotherapy can mean all things to all people. It is a bit like defining a human being as an animal and letting it go at that.

This extremely broad definition of psychotherapy is given because psychotherapy encompasses so many diff-

erent techniques that it is probably impossible to include
them all in a short definition. To illustrate this statement
and approach a more specific definition of psychotherapy, we can say that it usually involves some form of
communication between the therapist (the person practicing psychotherapy) and the patient. This communication is most often verbal. The therapist and the patient
sit and talk to each other about the patient's problems.

But a certain amount of the communication is nonver-
bal. Attitudes and emotions are also conveyed by facial
expressions, gestures, and physical reactions. There was
one therapist who used to take the patient in his lap and
cuddle him like a baby.

There are forms of psychotherapy, however, which
occasionally use avoidance of communication as a
method of treatment. In some instances the practitioners
of "operant therapy," which is based on the research of
Harvard University psychologist B. F. Skinner, have
achieved good results by deliberately not talking to the
patient.

Usually, the psychotherapist does not use any equipment in his treatment. He does not do anything to the
patient physically. The therapist and the patient (or patients, in the case of group therapy) just sit and talk. The
equipment consists of a chair or the famous couch so the
patient can be comfortable. But there are exceptions.
The operant therapists use equipment. They have
shown, for example, that they can both cause and cure
stammering by administering harmless but irritating
electric shocks to a person—of which more later in the
book.

But such equipment and treatment bears no resem-
blance to the medical treatment used or formerly used by
physicians in mental hospitals. In the past, though not

much any more, doctors sought to cure mental illness through surgery. In an operation called a lobotomy, surgeons inserted an implement in the head and severed part of the brain. Another form of medical treatment still used, although on a vastly reduced scale, is shock therapy. Patients are administered a large number of high voltage shocks to induce convulsions, a process that is alleged to be curative.

The medical treatment most used today is called *chemotherapy*. Patients are given a variety of pills, usually either tranquilizers or psychic-energizers. No responsible person believes these pills cure patients. But they do mask the symptoms of illness, make it easier for the patient to get on in the world, and make it easier for him to receive psychotherapy. Today great effort is being expended in hospitals and university laboratories to find physical causes for mental illness, which might lead to cures through pills or injections. Until or unless that happens, the principal, if not sole, method of treatment for the mentally deranged is psychotherapy.

On whom is psychotherapy used? Therapists have estimated that if 100 percent of the American population visited them for examination, they would feel that 95 percent would benefit from treatment. This is a way of saying that we are all a little bit crazy. But most of us manage to live reasonably successfully most of the time despite our fears, anxieties, prejudices, angers, blue moods or depressions, bad habits, aches and pains, alcoholic or drug excesses, laziness, and general aberrations from our usual or expected behavior.

A general statement may be made that psychotherapists treat or would like to treat those people who cannot live successfully under such rather normal conditions or who, while managing to get along in society, experience great discomfort themselves or cause it for other people.

The maladies therapists attempt to treat are of a wide variety. The major or gross symptoms are these: the person, because of a derangement of his thinking, wants to do violence to others or to himself; he has delusions, that is, he clings to an irrational belief despite all evidence to the contrary, (the classic example is the man who insists he is Napoleon); he has hallucinations, that is, he sees or hears nonexistent people or voices; he has chronic states of depression of long duration in which he is totally withdrawn into himself and unable or unwilling to communicate with or react to other people; he has manic states, that is, periods of frenzied activity and incessant chatter; and/or he exhibits such bizarre and antisocial behavior that it is impossible for other people and society to tolerate him. The latter category can include almost anything, but major examples are gross rages, sexual deviations, stealing, vandalism and other illegal acts, alcoholism and addiction, and extreme failure to abide by the rules of society or some subgroup in it.

Such persons are generally considered mentally ill. If the behavior is gross, the person will probably be institutionalized in a hospital or some other place for treatment. If the behavior is more tolerable to society, perhaps manifesting itself only occasionally, the person may live in the community while being treated as an outpatient at a hospital or clinic or undergo private treatment by a psychotherapist.

All people with gross behavioral symptoms are said to be suffering from a *psychosis*. People who endeavor to treat them have grouped several of the symptoms in an effort to classify types of illness, such as *paranoia* (feelings of persecution), *schizophrenia* (inability to tell the real from the unreal or simply inappropriate emotional reactions), *manic-depressive* states, and *character disorders* (gross antisocial behavior).

Most physicians and therapists have difficulty in classifying patients. The symptoms of each classification are so broad that depression, for example, may be a characteristic of each of them, along with agitation and a variety of strange behavior. A paranoid will have delusions and so will a schizophrenic. For this reason, there is an enlarging trend to do away with all efforts to classify patients in terms of specific illnesses. The terms frequently are meaningless, and they do not usually control the type of treatment given the person.

Therapists also—perhaps more often—treat a wide variety of less severe mental disorders. The term generally used for these is *neuroses* (plural of *neurosis*). This is another extremely broad, all-encompassing term. In general, it means that the person is suffering from considerable and persistent anxiety, tension and helplessness. He may be fear-ridden, experiencing frequent feelings that something dreadful is going to happen. He may have irrational fears (called *phobias*) of heights, enclosed places, blood, animals, or certain situations. He may be compulsive in his behavior, engaging in excessive and ritualistic acts which he is unable to control, preoccupied absurdly with cleanliness, diet fads, elaborate health precautions, or superstitions. Or he may have physical ailments induced by mental problems. Mild forms of such trouble may be indigestion, diarrhea, insomnia and headaches. In serious cases, the person may be unable to walk or speak. Such mentally induced conditions are called *psychosomatic illnesses*.

Such persons would be considered obvious neurotics.

Therapists try to treat large numbers of such people who appear perfectly normal and ordinary to all but their most intimate relatives and friends. Such neurotics may simply be unhappy, experiencing great discomfort in their family and social life and in their jobs. They may have marriage problems, sexual maladjustments, difficulty in making and keeping friends, problems in accomplishing simple tasks. They may make excessive use of alcohol, drugs or medicines. They may find it extremely difficult to resist urges to perform illegal, immoral or dangerous acts. Or they may be lacking in spontaneity and feel fearful, helpless and trapped. In short, the neurotic is anyone who is excessively and persistently unhappy, fearful and helpless and acts accordingly so that he is unproductive and unsuccessful at home, at work and in social relationships.

Since everyone has such feelings at least some of the time, it is important to emphasize that it is the persistent or chronic nature of such feelings and behavior that is abnormal. The neurotic simply seldom has feelings of well-being, self-satisfaction, contentment, accomplishment and happiness.

All of these people, psychotic and neurotic alike, go, want to go or perhaps ought to go to a psychotherapist. Who is he or she? Who practices psychotherapy? There are many types ranging from the most highly trained and knowledgeable to the untrained but enthusiastic.

The most prestigious and respected practitioner is the *psychiatrist*. He is a medical doctor who specializes in treating mental illness, just as other doctors specialize in surgery, internal medicine and pediatrics. The psychiatrist has had regular medical training, followed by two to four years of inservice experience as an interne and resident in hospitals. Any doctor can declare himself a psychiatrist, but almost without exception the real psychiatrist has specialized by spending his internship and certainly his residency in a mental hospital. He takes special courses in mental illness and psychotherapy and treats patients under the supervision of experienced psychiatrists.

Because of his medical training, the psychiatrist's exclusive province is that handful of mental diseases known to have physical causes. It is known that emotional and behavioral disorders can result from brain tumors, glandular disturbances, advanced syphilis, advanced alcoholism and addiction, mental retardation, some forms of brain dysfunction and certain other causes. These the psychiatrist treats.

The psychiatrist may or may not be a psychotherapist. He may deal exclusively with people suffering from the above-named physical disorders, as well as disorders of the central nervous system. In treating other types of mental patients—which is most of them—he may limit himself to chemotherapy, shock therapy and surgical techniques. He may never engage in the sort of verbal communication with a patient that is typical of psychotherapy, although it would be unusual if he did not attempt psychotherapy at least some of the time.

The criticism has been voiced many times, especially by psychiatrists themselves, that when he does attempt psychotherapy his training leaves him at a disadvantage. Because of his medical training, he has had relatively less time to study psychology and psychotherapeutic techniques. His training in these areas has been sporadic and part-time. Many of his techniques of psychotherapy have been learned in what amounts to on-the-job training after medical school. Many psychiatrists amend the deficiency by enrolling in special courses. There is agitation to improve psychiatric training by the introduction of more courses in psychology and psychotherapy in medical school.

The person who does have the training in these fields is the *clinical psychologist*. In most instances, he will have studied psychology as his college major, then gone on to earn a master's degree and a doctorate in the field of psychotherapy. During this period of post-graduate study and perhaps for a year or two afterwards, he will have received on-the-job training in mental institutions working with patients. Thus, the clinical psychologist who bears the letters "Ph.D." after his name will have engaged in eight to ten years of intensive study of psychology and psychotherapy.

One of the areas of controversy in the field of mental health is the friction between psychiatrists and clinical psychologists. The psychiatrist always has the higher rank and salary and greater prestige in a mental hospital or other institution. This fact is sometimes resented by clinical psychologists, who feel they have more training and expertise in psychotherapy.

The next most highly trained is the *psychologist*. He generally has a master's degree in the field. He may and often does accept patients for psychotherapy, but his special province is psychological testing. Over the years, psychology has developed a wide variety of tests to measure intelligence, aptitude—mechanical, artistic and verbal, and various traits of personality or character. Through testing, the psychologist tries to identify a person who has a mental disorder and to pinpoint its nature. Through tests and a personal interview, the psychologist might, for example, discover that serious emotional upsets are the root cause of a child's poor performance in school, a criminal's committing robberies or burglaries, a woman's marriage problems. He might then recommend psychotherapy.

A *psychiatric social worker* is usually a person who has a master's degree in social work with special training in psychology and psychotherapy. This person calls upon patients or the families of patients in their home and tries to help them resolve difficulties in the family, home, work or community. This work is considered vital to the full recovery of persons released from a mental hospital.

The *psychiatric nurse* is, as the name suggests, a registered nurse who has had special training to enable her (and him) to deal with the special problems of mental patients in institutions.

This list exhausts the professions marked by special training in psychotherapy, but it far from exhausts the list of people who endeavor to practice psychotherapy. Some form of it, at least some of the concepts of psychotherapy, are widely used by sociologists, marriage counselors, ordinary physicians, clergymen, lawyers and judges, guidance counselors and teachers, all of whom had their training in other fields.

Then there is a host of what are usually called *lay advisers*. These are people who are interested in and enthusiastic about some form of psychotherapy. Frequently, they were in psychotherapy themselves. Having profited and learned from it, they feel qualified to assist others.

The list of nonprofessional practitioners should also include many parents. Using child psychology books and other sources, they frequently endeavor to apply a few therapeutic techniques to their offspring.

No effort is made here to downgrade the efforts of nonprofessionally trained therapists. In many instances, their work compares favorably with that of psychiatrists and clinical psychologists. Carl Rogers, whose system of therapy we will encounter later in the book, is among those who believe that doctors, clergymen, teachers and ordinary citizens can learn to use his methods. Moreover, studies have shown that housewives, students, clergymen and other nonprofessionals can be very useful in mental institutions by acting as team leaders of groups of patients, taking case histories and simply talking to patients.

In his book *The Psychiatrists*, Professor Arnold A. Rogow entitled his opening chapter "The Crisis in American Psychiatry." He cited a long list of criticisms of psychiatry and psychotherapy made from within and without the profession. He also cited the general low esteem in which psychiatry is held by the public, certainly in contrast to the high respect it had a quarter century ago and longer. He described the growing tendency to lampoon and ridicule the profession in newspapers, plays, books, cartoons, movies and other such media.

In part, the crisis in psychotherapy (which in this book is being used as a term including all forms of treatment of mental disorders, including psychoanalysis) stems from the profession's long-standing penchant for controversy.

It may be said that argument and disagreement are important in every science. Physicists disagree over the wave theory of light, physicians over the causes of cancer, astronomers over the origin of the universe, anthropologists over the environmental-versus-hereditary influences upon man. In the physical sciences, such disagreements occur in the absence of firm facts. The various viewpoints are put forth as a *theory* or *hypothesis*. Due recognition is given to other theories. Little effort is made to ridicule opposing theories. The scientists rarely engage in public name-calling.

Since Freud, psychotherapy has had a pronounced tendency to engage in professional bloodletting. As we shall see, Freud often amended his own theories, yet he drove a number of his followers from the fold because they disagreed with him and sought to amend his theories. Each of these men founded his own system and school of psychotherapy and recruited and trained followers, some of whom later broke with them. Psychotherapy has been at it ever since, proliferating into more and more systems.

There would be nothing wrong in this proliferation if an attitude of cooperation existed among the practitioners. But all too often it does not. Especially among the Freudian and Neo-Freudian psychoanalysts, there is a pronounced tendency for each to assume he has the whole and only truth and to scoff at or at least denigrate other theories and methods. The infighting among therapists in universities, mental institutions and professional societies becomes rather disabling at times.

Unfortunately, these disagreements make headlines. Questions of sanity and fitness to stand trial are frequently important in criminal cases. For decades, the public has been treated to the spectacle of the prosecution putting a battery of psychiatrists and psychologists on the stand who declare the defendant sane and able to stand trial, while the defense mounts another succession of equally qualified experts who say the opposite. The public is left to conclude that the whole passel of them are either corrupt or ignoramuses or that perhaps the whole subject of psychotherapy is a fraud.

Leaders of the profession are concerned about the image the public receives of the profession at these trials.

In his book *The Crime of Punishment,* Dr. Karl Menninger urged that all psychiatrists be excluded from the courtroom. "Put us all out and make us stay out," he wrote. "After you have tried the case, let us doctors and assistants examine him and confer together outside the courtroom and make a report to you which will express our view of the offender—his potentialities, his liabilities and the possible remedies."

Much of the controversy in the field of mental health stems from the simple fact that doctors and psychologists are working with one of the great unknowns of science, the human brain. After years of intensive study, researchers have pinpointed a few areas of the brain that seem to control such sensory functions as speech and some motor functions, such as walking. There is a growing—although far from complete—understanding of the structure of brain cells and the electrical and chemical means by which they function.

But some of the most important brain activities, including thought, memory, intelligence and emotion remain nearly total mysteries to the ablest researchers. These are the main ingredients which form what is usually called character or personality. They are also the stuff of psychotherapy.

When a scientist, or indeed any person, tries to understand something unknown, one method is to compare it to something known. For example, if a person wished to understand how the brain works, which is unknown, he might begin his investigation by assuming it works like a computer, which is known. Using the computer as a model, he would study the brain. If he discovered that the brain does not work like a computer, he would discard it as a model and use another one. By this method he would accumulate a great deal of negative and positive information about the brain and move closer to understanding how it works.

Faced with the great unknown of the human mind and its emotions, man has through the ages used four different models in his effort to understand it. First and longest used was the *demon model*. Deranged persons whose behavior was socially unacceptable were assumed to be invaded by evil spirits or the devil. Treatment consisted of efforts to drive the evil spirit away. At best, treatment consisted of incantations, frightening images, strong purgatives and bloodletting. At worst, particularly in the Middle Ages, treatment aimed to make the body an inhospitable place for the evil spirit. The "demonized" person was beaten, burned, branded with hot irons, tortured, starved, imprisoned in dank dungeons in chains, and, if all else failed, burned at the stake as a witch. This sort of treatment went on for a thousand years or more.

In the nineteenth century, reformers convinced society of the inhumanity of such savage treatment. A key individual was Philippe Pinel, a Frenchman. In a famous experiment in the 1790s, he proved that if inmates were removed from the dungeons, placed in clean sunny rooms, well fed and treated kindly many would get well, even though they had been considered hopelessly mad for years. Other reformers took up the cause in Britain and the United States, which led to the use of what might be called the *moral model* in treatment.

Under this method inmates were treated with utmost kindness, frequently being housed in rural "retreats." Therapists assumed the inmate was misguided and had departed from the paths of morality and correct behavior. He was given a generous hearing of his problems, then a talking to about morality and ethics. There was emphasis on religion. Such treatment may seem rather simplistic today, but records show that in the last half of the last century it was highly successful. Institutions in England and the United States using moral therapy released two-thirds to three-quarters of their patients as improved or cured. This record has only recently been equaled in modern mental hospitals through massive use of tranquilizers and other pills. As we have already pointed out, these drugs do not cure the patient but only mask his symptoms.

The moral model, despite its success, was rather abruptly discarded for the *medical model*, which is overwhelmingly popular today. Starting just prior to this century and accelerating ever since, the theory is that the deranged person can be assumed to be mentally ill, just as a person can be physically ill with fevers, infection, cancer, heart disease and a host of other physical maladies.

Use of the medical model was encouraged by the startling advances in medicine and other physical sciences in the last half the Nineteenth century. Man came to understand the nature of energy, matter and electricity. In medicine, the basic mechanisms of the human body came to be understood, along with the bacterial nature of infection. There were many other advances, including anesthetics and surgery. For the fledgling science of psychiatry, an important discovery came in 1905 when it was found that advanced syphilis, a physical disease, causes mental derangement. Hope was born that physical causes could be found for other mental disorders.

The deranged were termed sick and considered patients. Such terms as mad, crazy or lunatic were discarded. Asylums were declared hospitals and designed along those lines. The persons treating patients became doctors and nurses. The various behaviors of patients, such as delusions, hallucinations, agitations, or depressions, were called symptoms of disease and names were attached to groups of symptoms so the patient could be said to be suffering from a specific disease.

Treatments were developed for the various diseases, including surgery, insulin or electric shock to induce convulsions, cold baths and others. As observed, the release rate in mental hospitals dwindled to a fraction of what it had been under moral therapy, but it began to rise again following World War II when chemotherapy began.

Simultaneously, systems of psychotherapy using the medical model were developed. Beginning in the 1890s and continuing until the 1930s, Sigmund Freud, a physician by training, developed a theory of the mind which sought to explain both normal and abnormal behavior. He developed a method for treating abnormalities. Many others also developed theories and methods that departed from Freud in small or larger ways, but all assumed aberrated or uncomfortable people were sick and used the medical model.

The fourth approach used to understand the human mind and its derangement is the *learning model*. The aberrated person is assumed to have learned incorrect or self-defeating modes of behavior, and therefore the object of his therapy is to induce him to unlearn his past methods and relearn more constructive ones. Here the therapist is not a doctor; he is a teacher.

Advocates of the various "learning" or "behavioral" therapies trace their origins back to the turn of the century and the work of the Russian scientist Ivan Pavlov.

He discovered what became known as the *conditioned reflex* by teaching dogs to salivate at the sound of a bell rather than at the sight or smell of food. In the following decades psychologists developed a variety of theories to explain how a person learns. These theories were based on scientific research with animals and later humans.

Other psychologists began to apply these learning theories to persons with mental disorders. Unlike the Freudians or others who use some form of therapy which attempts to give the person insight into the causes of his problems, the learning therapists are little interested in the past events in the person's life or in his motivations. They never ask the patient why he does something. They wish only to know what he does. Then they seek to teach him a more useful way of behaving. It is not getting ahead of our story to say the teaching is done through some form of *reinforcement.* Ways are found to reward the patient for desired behavior. Occasionally he may be punished for undesired behavior.

The major controversy in psychotherapy today and for the foreseeable future is between the Freudians and other insight therapists and the learning therapists. It is a battle royal. The insight therapists, who quarrel among themselves over their various theories and methods, can agree in their opposition to the learning therapies. The learning therapists, perhaps because they are a small minority in the profession, are more tolerant of each other's theories and thus more united.

In pages to come we will discuss in detail the alleged virtues and criticisms of these two approaches to psychotherapy. Suffice it to say at this point that the learning therapists consider the insight therapists to be grossly unscientific, offering theories that are patently unprovable and thereby unsupportable by evidence. The insight therapists consider the learning therapists to be mechanistic, dehumanizing man, the only animal capable of conscious thought and emotion, to the level of rats, cats and dogs.

2

Freud's Early Theories

Many consider Sigmund Freud, the father of modern psychotherapy, to be one of the most influential men of science in history. He must rank with Copernicus and Galileo in astronomy, Newton and Einstein in physics, Darwin in biology, Mendel in genetics, who greatly altered man's understanding of his environment. All of these men (save Einstein, as yet) have been proved wrong in part of their theories. But their highly original concepts spurred other men to continue their studies. All were men of influence far beyond their times.

Freud gave man a whole new way of looking at himself. He offered theories that sought to explain the working of the mind, its motivations, habits, behavior and thoughts. Freud's theories have had a profound influence throughout most of this century on psychology and psychiatry, medicine, literature, the theater, the arts, education, child rearing, the laws and courts, politics, indeed, the full social fabric of American life. Whether one agrees with the changes or not, it must be said that our entire moral structure in America today, including "permissiveness," "the generation gap," and changed attitudes toward sex and religion, are based in large measure upon Freud's concepts and public understanding (or misunderstanding) of his teachings.

Freud was born in Freiberg, Moravia, now part of East Germany, in 1856. His family moved to Vienna, Austria, when he was three years old, where he remained until 1936. At that time, he fled to London to escape the anti-Jewish pogroms of Nazi Germany and died in England in 1939 at the age of 83. His long, work-filled life thus spanned an era of fantastic scientific and technological change. Darwin's *Origin of Species* was published when Freud was three. This revolutionized man's attitudes towards himself by showing that man was an animal and therefore an object for scientific study. When Freud was four, Gustav Fechner founded the science of psychology by demonstrating that the mental processes of man could be brought into the laboratory and accurately measured.

Freud grew up with and was profoundly impressed by the theories and discoveries that revolutionized the physical sciences. In the middle of the nineteenth century, the German physicist Hermann von Helmholtz had formulated the principle of conservation of energy. Energy cannot be destroyed. When it disappears in one form, Helmholtz said, it appears in another.

This principle led to discovery after discovery of the nature and use of energy—thermodynamics, the electromagnetic field, radioactivity, the electron, the quantum theory, and Einstein's theory of relativity. All of today's electrical and motorized gadgetry stems from such studies, from the electric motor to the computer, from the internal combustion engine to the jet airplane, from atomic structure to atomic bombs.

Freud's life spanned most of these discoveries. As a young medical student in the 1870s, he studied under Ernst Brücke at the University of Vienna. Brücke taught a then radical theory that the living organism is a dynamic system in which the laws of chemistry and physics apply. We take the first step toward understanding Freud's theories when we realize that he ultimately came to apply the principles of chemistry, physics and conservation of energy to the human personality. He designed a "dynamic" theory of psychology in which the transformations and exchanges of energy within the personality are the key to understanding its workings.

Freud wanted to be not a doctor but a scientist. He was interested in the physiology or anatomical structure of the human nervous system and for some years did research in that area at the University of Vienna. He made no particularly important discoveries, but he gained experience in scientific methods of study. Ultimately, he had to enter the practice of medicine for financial reasons. He could not support his growing family on the meager salary at the University. Anti-semitism in Vienna kept him from being promoted to higher-paying positions.

When Freud began to practice medicine, it was natural, with his background, that he would specialize in nervous disorders. He began to see a number of patients who suffered from "hysteria." The term is no longer commonly used in psychology, but in those days it was a catch-all term for such symptoms as paralyzed limbs, deafness, blindness and other conditions for which no medical cause could be found. Today the term "psychosomatic illness" is used for such ailments.

Freud searched for a way to treat hysterical patients. He learned of the work of the great French neurologist Jean Martin Charcot. He was experimenting with *hypnosis* to treat hysteria. Hypnosis is a sleeplike condition induced by another person in which the patient loses consciousness but is able to respond to suggestions by the hypnotist by talking, walking and making other movements. Freud went to Paris in 1885 and studied under Charcot for about a year.

He returned to Vienna somewhat disenchanted with hypnosis as a method of treatment. He found it only occasionally successful. Not all patients could be hypnotised, and even when they were the treatment was not always beneficial.

Back in Vienna, Freud began to work with another Viennese physician, Joseph Breuer. The two men found that some hysteria patients could be helped by having them "talk out" their problems while under hypnosis. Soon the two doctors abandoned hypnosis and used the talking out process in the waking state. The patient would pour out his problems, while Breuer or Freud listened and made notes. Many patients seemed to feel better after pent-up feelings were poured forth in the process known as *catharsis*.

The two men published their findings in a 1893 paper entitled *Studies in Hysteria*. Shortly afterwards they ceased to collaborate and went separate ways. The reasons for this breakup would plague Freud the rest of his life and to a lesser extent his followers to this day. Breuer had disliked two elements in the treatment. The patients seemed to form a pronounced emotional attachment to the therapist. This made Breuer uncomfortable. Worse, from his standpoint, much of the pent-up talk that poured out of the patients dealt with sex. Breuer was personally embarrassed. Freud, perhaps because of his training in scientific observation, felt that both the sexual content and the emotional attachment to the therapist (later to be called *transference*, because the patient transfers his feelings about someone else to the therapist) were of utmost importance. His theories developed out of these two observations.

Ultimately, Freud came to explain personality development largely in terms of sex and to describe mental or emotional disorders in terms of incorrect or incomplete sexual development. In those days, the 1890s, the word sex wasn't even used in polite company. It was the Victorian Era of rigid manners, excessive modesty, high moral standards and lofty ideals. To suggest, as Freud did, that men and women—let alone children—had an inordinate interest in sex was to engage in the most prurient of speech. Freud was roundly denounced in a controversy that raged around the world. It was abated only by the greater concerns of World War I in 1914.

After breaking off with Breuer, Freud worked pretty much alone for several years, analysing himself as well as patients, developing his theories and techniques of analysis, as well as writing. His first major work was *The Interpretation of Dreams*. It was published in 1900 but had been written some years before. It was not well received by the scientific community, but Freud was unfazed. In 1904, he published *The Psychopathology of Everyday Life*, followed the next year by *A Case of Hysteria, Three Essays on Hysteria*, and *Wit and Its Relation to the Unconscious*.

Shortly after the turn of the century, Freud's writings and his successful treatment of patients through psychoanalysis began to attract followers, including Alfred Adler, Carl Jung, Wilhelm Stekel, Otto Rank and Sandor Ferenczi. They organized a seminar for the study of psychoanalytical techniques. A scientific journal devoted to psychoanalysis was published, and the Viennese Psychoanalytic Society was formed.

In 1909, Freud received his first academic recognition when he was invited to speak at Clark University in Worcester, Massachusetts. Stanley Hall, the president of the university and a distinguished psychologist, recognized the importance of Freud's work and helped to promote his views in the United States.

Freud's fame grew. By the 1920s, Freud and his theories were an international sensation. Psychoanalysis became the rage. The "in" thing was to be psychoanalyzed. Fashionable people felt compelled to discuss such words as subconscious, inhibitions, complexes, repressed urges and, of course, sex, which fueled popular enthusiasm for Freud's work. Sex had been a forbidden subject for a long time. Millions of people seized the opportunity to discuss the subject as a scientific and medical phenomenon. Freud's theories also had wide influence in the 1920s on art, literature, religion, morals, education, social customs and other aspects of life. Criticism and even ridicule of Freud's theories existed, but it tended to be lost in the wholehearted public acceptance of his ideas.

What was all the shouting about? No attempt will be made here to present Freud's theories in an exact historical fashion. Rather, the effort is to make them understandable, while maintaining a thread of historical development. It is important to remember that Freud did not develop *a* theory, but *several* theories, or better said, he kept changing and expanding his theory on the basis of information, observation and thought.

Freud believed there was a reason for everything a person does. There is no such thing as an accident or a coincidence. If a person stubs his toe, has an accident and

is injured or injures someone else, drops a glass, gets
drunk, has something "on the tip of his tongue" and
can't think of it, or makes a misstatement as a "slip of the
tongue," there is a reason for it, even though the person
does not know the reason and assumes it was an accident
or coincidence. Freud believed that even jokes and sense
of humor had a cause.

The cause lay in the *unconscious mind*. The mind is like
an iceberg. As everyone knows, only a small part of an
iceberg is visible above the surface of the water. A vastly
larger amount is invisible below the surface. The visible
part of the iceberg can be likened to the *conscious* mind.
It contains that which we know and can remember and
the thought processes by which we seem to function.
Below the surface of awareness is the vastly larger unconscious mind. It contains everything we ever learned,
knew, felt or experienced which we have "forgotten."
Some of this material may be truly forgotten because it
is trivial and unimportant or was not properly learned
in the first place. Thus, an adult may have forgotten a
poem he memorized as a child or how to figure algebraic
equations which he once knew simply because he has
little need to know or to use it. A woman of my acquaint-
ance grew up in a French-speaking home and could
speak the language fluently at age five. Thereafter, she
moved into an English-speaking home. When she studied French in high school, she no longer remembered
any of it and had to relearn from the beginning.

But much that is in the unconscious mind which we
cannot remember has been deliberately suppressed,
Freud believed, because the memory would be unpleasant. An example would be a child who saw an automobile accident. The blood and screams might be so unpleasant a memory that the child would suppress or, in

Freudian terms, *repress* them into the unconscious. He would have no conscious memory of the accident.

Freud believed the mind was a self-enclosed energy system. The memories repressed into the unconscious have energy or power and are constantly seeking to reach the surface or consciousness. And they do, but in altered form. The forgotten accident of childhood might manifest itself in a fear of blood, cars, travel or enclosed places. In certain circumstances it might take the form of high-speed, reckless driving or a sadistic preoccupation with blood and death. To Freud, the whole point of psychotherapy was to bring to consciousness that content of the unconscious mind which was unpleasant and caused painful, self-defeating or neurotic behavior. When the person was consciously aware of this forgotten material, he could understand it and his reactions to it and resolve the problems resulting from it in a more satisfactory manner.

Freud's theory was that the unconscious mind revealed itself in a number of ways. One, as already mentioned, was through misstatements, accidents and coincidences. A second manifestation was in dreams. When the person sleeps and his conscious mind is resting, the material in the unconscious boils to the surface, but again in altered forms. The repressed accident might come out as a dream about a waterfall or flood, for example. It might be almost anything. A major function of the analyst, in Freud's view, is to interpret dreams. When a person dreams about water, say, he really may mean blood. Freud believed his work in the interpretation of dreams to be his most important contribution to psychology.

Before he could realistically interpret a dream, however, Freud had to have a general idea of the content of

the unconscious. For this purpose he began to use a
technique known as *free association.* The patient was
stretched out in a comfortable position on a couch and
encouraged to say without restraint, inhibition or fear
anything that came into his head. The patient was not to
censor his words in any way or say what he felt he ought
to or was expected to say. He simply uttered whatever
came to mind.

Freud took a seat at the head of the couch, out of the
patient's view. In free association, Freud was largely
silent, limiting his remarks to encouraging the patient
when he felt censorship had occurred. Freud remained
impersonal. He revealed nothing of himself to the patient, made no attempt to form any sort of relationship
with him at all, and made no value judgments of the
patient or his utterances. He sought to be a disembodied
presence without personality.

Free association went on for an hour at a time, five
days a week. After several weeks or months, a pattern of
censorship began to reveal itself. Whenever the patient
was about to say something, he would become silent, or
abruptly change the subject, or say he couldn't remember. In time, Freud saw that this always occurred about
the same subject matter. By deduction or intuition,
Freud surmised the nature of this unutterable material.
Gradually, Freud would become more active, returning
the patient to the suppressed subject matter and encouraging him to associate freely about it.

As this process went on, another technique for revealing the unconscious came to be used. The patient came
to have strong emotional feelings about Freud, including
anger, hate, love or dependence. But it will be remembered that Freud had been acting as a nonperson all this
time. Revealing nothing of himself, not even being visi-

ble for the most part, he obviously had done nothing to warrant such feelings. Freud concluded that the patient was engaging in *transference*, that is, he was transferring to Freud the unconscious feelings he had about someone else. Thus, if the patient demonstrated hostility, hatred or fear toward Freud, he might conclude the patient actually had such unconscious feeling toward someone else, his father for example. By observing the patient's mistakes and accidents, interpreting his dreams, listening to his free association and observing his transference, Freud learned to map the patient's unconscious. Treatment came to be helping the patient make a conscious and emotional resolution of this unconscious material.

It is commonly thought that Freud discovered the unconscious mind. He did not. Others had written about unconscious processes prior to him. Freud's contribution was in explaining the uses of the unconscious, the means by which material is repressed and how the contents of the unconscious may be revealed, and especially the general nature of unconscious material.

Freud theorized that human beings have two vital drives, the drive for self-preservation and the drive toward procreation, that is, preservation of the species. The desire for self-preservation is of little concern, because it is seldom thwarted. The problem takes care of itself. The other drive, which Freud called the *libido* or sexual energy, was something else. It was constantly being thwarted by other people and by society, creating great difficulties for people.

Freud gave a special meaning to the word *sex*, as explained by British psychiatrist Dr. J. A. C. Brown in his book *Freud and the Post-Freudians:*

Originally Freud, when he used the word "sex," meant it to be understood in the ordinary everyday sense, but about this time he decided to use it in a much wider connotation to apply to any pleasurable sensation relating to the body functions, and also . . . to such feelings as tenderness, pleasure in work and friendship. In other words, he used the word to refer to what would ordinarily be described as "desire."

It is to be doubted, however, that most people who discuss Freud's theories of sex put this broader meaning on the word.

Do you remember that Breuer had broken with Freud over the sexual content of the material learned from carthasis? The sheer volume of talk about sex and sexual experiences led Freud to conclude first that neuroses were a result of childhood sexual experiences. Possibly the child had been sexually seduced by an adult. Sometimes the child might have been an active participant in the sexual relations. Sometimes he might have been inactive, or passive.

Freud soon had to abandon this theory. From conversations with patients' parents and members of their families, Freud learned that the events described by patients simply had not occurred. The patients were making it up. They were fantasizing.

At first this information seemed to strike a fatal blow to Freud's work, but he tenaciously struggled for answers to the question why so many patients would imagine themselves to have been the object of sexual seduction by a parent. From his belief that all physical and mental activity has a cause and from his belief that fears are frequently the expression of unconscious desires, Freud formulated two theories: *infantile sexuality* and the *Oedipus complex.*

The child is born with a libido or sexual energy. It is an instinct. Its first expression is *oral.* According to Freud, the infant derives great pleasure through the mouth, by suckling at his mother's breast or from a bottle. He constantly puts his hand or other objects in his mouth. From about age one to three, the child enters what Freud called the *anal* stage, deriving pleasure from retention and expulsion of feces. During this phase, the child's interests are largely concentrated on himself (narcissism) and satisfactions are derived chiefly from his own body.

Somewhere between ages three and seven, the child enters the *phallic* stage in which the energy of the libido centers on the penis in the male, the clitoris in the female. At first, the child finds pleasure in these organs, but soon the sexual interest centers on the parents, ushering in the Oedipal period.

Freud derived the term Oedipus from the Greek play by Sophocles, *Oedipus Rex,* in which Oedipus unknowingly murders his father and marries his mother. The gods, as punishment, visit a plague upon the Greek city-state of Thebes. Freud applied this general theme to a child's relationship with his parents. No part of Freud's theories has had greater influence or been more roundly denounced.

In the case of boys, according to Freud, the young child develops a sexual interest in his mother and a sense of rivalry with his father over his mother's affections. He longs to take his father's place beside his mother. Freud maintained that the child soon learns that such desires are forbidden. He experiences complex emotions of love and hate for his father and develops strong feelings of fear and guilt. More, the child expects to be punished by his father for his incestuous desires for his mother, and the form of punishment most expected or feared is castration, that is, to lose his penis *(castration complex)*. In Freud's interpretation, the Oedipus complex in males is resolved by the castration complex, that is, the boy's fear of castration forces him to surrender his desire for his mother.

In the case of little girls, the situation is more complex. Freud never was able to make it entirely clear. The girl is said to have an *Electra Complex*, from a Greek myth in which Electra connives to kill her mother Clytemnestra, who had murdered her father Agamemnon. As in the case of boys, the little girl's first object of attachment is her mother. Freud believed both the oral and anal stages had a strong phallic orientation among girls. According to him, she becomes interested in her clitoris as the biological equivilent to the boy's penis, but since it is much smaller, she desires to be like the boy. Freud called this *penis envy*. Freud maintained that the girl next develops an attachment to her father and a hatred and fear of her mother. This is complicated by the fact that the girl, having no penis, feels she has already been punished for her incestuous desires. Her conflict is resolved when she renounces the hope of masculinity and accepts castration as a fact of life.

Freud believed that unsuccessful resolution of the Oedipal and Electra complexes led to neurotic difficulties in adult life. The incestuous desires, instead of being resolved by age five, as is normal, continue. But the guilt and fears resulting from the desires are too awful to bear, so the desires are buried deep into the unconscious, from which they emerge as other, seemingly unrelated, problems.

Under Freud's theory, the child remains in the phallic state until about age twelve, but from age seven on he is in a period of *latency*. His libido continues to grow, but its nature is not greatly changed. Then, at age twelve, when the child enters puberty and glandular changes occur in the body, there is a great increase in sexual energy. If the child has made a relatively successful resolution of the Oedipal complex, the sexual interest is transferred to a person of the opposite sex. The person enters the final, or *genital*, stage of successful adulthood and normal sexual relationships.

If, however, the Oedipal conflict was not successfully resolved or there are other emotional problems, the person may regress to earlier oral or anal stages where he had adjusted more successfully.

Freud postulated a number of attributes that he maintained are characteristic of persons with oral or anal characters. They cannot all be listed here, but an oral person may make excessive use of tobacco, alcohol or food; seek to acquire these things through symbolic means, such as money, power or material possessions; talk a lot; be nasty and sarcastic in his speech or be socially dependent upon other people, emulating the dependence he had upon his mother to feed and care for him when he was a baby. Or, he may do the opposite and feel obliged to help others through social work, medicine or the ministry.

In the anal stage, the adult may develop qualities based upon his experiences during toilet training. If his mother was very strict and punished him when he soiled himself, the adult may rebel against authority by being messy, irresponsible, disorderly, wasteful and extravagant. Or there may be an opposite reaction of excessive neatness, compulsive orderliness, fear of dirt and frugality with money. If the mother extravagantly praised the child when he had a bowel movement in the toilet, the adult stuck in this phase may be motivated to create things to please other people. If too much emphasis was placed by the mother upon bowel movements, the child may have felt that he had lost something valuable down the drain. As an adult, therefore, he may be overly thrifty and derive pleasure from collecting, owning and hoarding objects.

In short, Freud believed at this early stage of his work that neurotic and other emotional disorders were caused by unsuccessful sexual development. The patient had not progressed through the oral, anal and phallic stages to the genital. His progress had been blocked somewhere along the line. Or, having made the adjustment, some emotional experience had caused him to regress to an earlier stage. In either event, the cause was sexual. The aim of psychoanalysis came to be to dredge out of the unconscious mind that "forgotten" material which would illuminate the sexual experiences or lack of them and the sexual desires that caused neurotic behavior.

One more point is important. Because Freud saw the libido as energy and the psychic system as a self-contained one, any sort of change in surface behavior was self-defeating, unless the underlying sexual cause was corrected. Thus, an oral person might give up smoking only to indulge in overeating. A man with a strong attachment to his mother might break away and marry, only to put himself in a dependent relationship with his wife, expecting her to mother him.

Freud did not abandon these theories, but in the 1920s he altered and expanded them into a new theory of the mind and its functions. It is this we take up in the next chapter.

3

Freud's Later Theories

Freud's theories of infant sexualism as an explanation for personality development and mental disorders created a world-wide sensation. Every informed person, and a good many uninformed ones, talked about them. The theories were accepted in toto by many people, including large numbers of influential psychologists and psychiatrists. Indeed, when most nonexperts speak today of Freudian analysis, they probably have in mind these early theories of Freud.

There was a lot of disagreement, however. Many people found it rather difficult to accept the notion that babies and toddlers went around lusting after their parents. Some of Freud's closest associates, starting with Alfred Adler in 1911, broke with Freud over the sex issue. Adler and the others could not believe that infant sex was the only—or even the primary—cause for mental disorders. Thus was begun the schism in the ranks of psychoanalysis. It has only intensified since.

Freud himself soon altered his theories. A major factor was his observation that the terrifying dreams of battle-shocked soldiers in World War I could hardly be explained in terms of sex and wish fulfillment. He concluded that aggressive feelings, as well as sex, were an important instinct subject to repression in the unconscious. This led him, after 1920, to develop a new theory of personality.

As fully developed, Freud's theory hypothesized that man has two basic instincts, a life instinct or *Eros* and a death instinct or *Thanatos.* The latter is also known as *mortido* or *destrudo.* The life instinct consists of the old concept of libido and part of the self-preservation drive. The death instinct is an innate destructiveness and aggression directed against the self. It is a drive constantly working towards death, when man returns to his original inorganic state of complete freedom from tension or striving.

Freud concluded that the dreams of soldiers, in which they repeatedly reenacted some horrible experience in the war, were related to the tendency of the death instinct to return the mind to earlier states. This concept has been largely rejected by Freudians today. Most psychiatrists believe that dreams are an effort of the mind to accept and adjust to an experience it formerly found intolerable.

Since inwardly directed aggression is dangerous to the individual, Freud went on, the mind attempts to make it less destructive. This is done either by erotizing it, that is, combining it with the libido to take the form of sadism or masochism (sexual conduct in which sex and aggression are combined and used against other people or oneself) or by directing the aggression against others. Freud believed that suicide represented a breakdown of these two defense procedures. He also felt that such phenomena as accidents, self-inflicted diseases, addictions and poorly executed criminal acts that led the offender to be caught easily were further breakdowns in defense against the death instinct.

This theory, which appeared in 1922, was greeted with a storm of protest, even among Freud's most devoted followers. Today his account of aggression is generally accepted among psychoanalysts, but little reference is made to his life or death instinct.

Freud then proposed a new theory of personality in which he downgraded the importance of the unconscious and substituted a three-way division of the mind into the Id, Ego and Superego.

The mind of the newborn child is solely *id*, that is, it is a seething mass of impulses or instinctive drives entirely lacking conscious control. The id is the depository of all the animalistic instincts accumulated through the ages, such as shutting the eyes before a bright light, blinking, hunger, thirst, sex and many others. The sole function of the id is to provide for the immediate discharge of energy or tension that is created by stimulation. Thus, the baby shuts its eyes before a bright light to end the stimulation of the retina of the eye. The contraction of the stomach muscles caused by hunger leads the baby to discharge the tension by crying. Freud saw the id working on the *pleasure principle*. Its aim is instant gratification of pleasure by eliminating tension or at least keeping it at the lowest possible level.

But not all tensions can be relieved immediately. The baby has no ability to feed himself. If the parents do not feed him, he will starve. Or, if the parents fail to interpret correctly his crying or if they impose on him rigid schedules of feeding that are unrelated to his hunger, the id will remain in a state of frustrated tension.

The id then engages in what Freud termed the *primary process*. The id substitutes a memory image for the actual thing. To illustrate, the Id cannot differentiate between food and the memory of food. This memory may be based upon the experience of having food in the past or the id may already possess the image at birth. An illustration of the primary process, Freud believed, was the hungry man who dreams of food or the sexually aroused person who has erotic dreams. The id is releasing tensions through the image rather than the fact. Rather obviously, images are a poor substitute for actual food, making the primary process rather ineffectual as a tension reliever.

The id, stemming as it does from our ancient animal past, is unchanging. It has no contact with external reality, so it cannot learn or be improved or altered in any way. It is entirely without organization, and its source of energy can flow from instinct to instinct at will. More, the id remains infantile throughout the person's life. It continues to seek immediate gratification and relief of tensions. As psychologist Calvin S. Hall said in *A Primer of Freudian Psychology*, the id is "demanding, impulsive, irrational, asocial, selfish and pleasure-loving. It is the spoiled child of the personality. It is omnipotent because it has the magical power of fulfilling its wishes by imagination, fantasy, hallucinations and dreams."

Freud believed the id accounted for the impulses people have to commit aggressive or sexual acts, for the mindless pursuit of a pretty girl or handsome guy, for irrational acts of vandalism or violence.

The *ego* develops from the id as a result of the ineffectiveness of images as gratifications for desires or needs. A hungry person must have actual food. He cannot live on a memory of food. Thus, the person must learn what food is. He cannot long go around indiscriminately sticking things in his mouth in hopes they are edible. He must also learn how to obtain food. The ego develops out of the discovery that impulsive behavior, such as a temper tantrum, can call forth parental punishment leading to an increase, not a decrease, in tensions.

The id is governed by the pleasure principle, the ego by the *reality principle*. As the child ages and engages in thought, he learns to differentiate the real from the imaginary—actual food, for example, He learns to plan ahead to obtain whatever will provide gratification for the instinctive desires. Such planning may involve some postponement of gratification, putting up with some tension or discomfort, to achieve a realistic gratification. To give a simple example, a child learns that if he doesn't eat everytime he feels like it and endures some discomfort, he will receive a large amount of food at dinner, perhaps topped off with a dessert. He will also win parental approval for his good eating habits, which is pleasant.

The ego operates on the *secondary process,* as Freud called it. The primary process only produces an image of what will satisfy a need. The secondary process works out a plan of action to achieve the satisfaction. In a word, the secondary process is thought or problem-solving. And, if one plan doesn't work, another is developed to accomplish the purpose.

A well-adjusted person's ego continues to grow in strength as he matures in age and knowledge. He learns to make ever finer distinctions between the real and the unreal, to develop more effective plans of action, to postpone gratifications to achieve ever greater satisfactions, to control the destructive impulses of the id. To a certain extent, the abilities of the ego are a result of heredity, that is, the person has certain physical or mental capabilities. But good use of these abilities through education and self-discipline is a sign of a strong ego and a well-adjusted person.

The *superego* develops out of the ego and is roughly identical to conscience. The child learns standards of moral conduct and correct behavior from his parents. The teaching may take the form of punishment, such as a spanking, being sent to his room, or being deprived of a pleasure (creating tension all), or through psychological means, such as scoldings or disapproving looks. In either event, the parent is withholding love from the child or causing the child to fear that his behavior may cause the parent not to love him.

The child learns quickly the moral and behavioral standards of his parents. In effect, he adopts *their* superegos. If the parents prize neatness and punish the child when he is untidy, he comes to value neatness. If truthfulness results in a pleasant experience and lying in an unpleasant one, truthfulness becomes an attribute of the child's superego. A large skein of values is built up in this way.

If the superego is to be effective, it must have the same ability the parents have to reward or punish—and it does, applying both to the ego, which is the part of the mind controlling actions and thought. If the ego performs in accordance with the superego's standards, it is rewarded with a feeling of pride and well-being. If it does not, the ego is punished, actually punished.

To illustrate: Suppose truthfulness is approved of by the superego and lying is not. If the ego tells the truth, even though physical punishment may be the result, it is rewarded with a feeling of self-esteem. If the ego lies, however, punishment will surely come in some form—an upset stomach, an accident, a mistake, loss of something valuable. This, of course, was Freud's new method of accounting for the mistakes, accidents and coincidences that fascinated him.

The id and the superego are alike in several ways. Neither has control over actions or conscious processes. Both are unreasoning, demanding and unchanging. And neither can differentiate between the real and the unreal. To the superego the mere thought of lying is the same as lying, even if the truth is ultimately to be uttered. Punishment, Freud believed, is inflicted for the thought as well as for the deed.

Most of the content of the superego comes from parents, but there are other sources, including policemen, teachers, clergymen and other authority figures, books, movies and other sources of moral and behavioral standards.

What is the function of the superego? It acts as a controlling force upon those aggressive and sexual impulses of the id which, if unchecked, would have most harmful effects upon the individual and society. Unchecked aggression could lead to imprisonment and death. Unchecked sexual activity could lead to a breakdown of the family and the whole structure of society.

Some Freudians state that the superego is the successor to the Oedipal complex. The fears and moral abhorrence of the Oedipal desires gives rise to the superego. In another exercise demonstrating his low regard for women, Freud theorized that women have a weak superego because they had to accept castration as an accepted fact of life. The allegedly inadequate moral nature of women was supposedly symbolized by Eve, who could not resist the apple in the Garden of Eden, with resultant problems for men ever since.

Freud saw the human personality as a sort of three-cornered struggle between the id, the superego and the external world in which the ego endeavors to live and act. The ego itself possesses no psychic energy, but it endeavors to take the energy of the id and transform it into realistic actions that will be acceptable gratifications to the id. In this task the ego is often thwarted by the superego, which is itself highly demanding and unreasonable. The ego thus must find a way to repress and satisfy the id impulses while not incurring the punishments meted out by the superego.

It is believed to be possible to see individuals wherein the ego is not faring too well in the struggle. The id-dominated person is impulsive, thoughtless, selfish, given to instant gratifications of the senses and motivated by pleasure. He may be quite juvenile, unproductive, self-defeating and in trouble with the law and society. The superego-dominated person suffers from an excess of conscience. He is rigid, timid, fearful, and lacking in spontaneity. He lacks courage and does not take risks. The person with the strong ego is well adjusted. He is neither impulsive or unduly restricted, a useful blend of spontaneity and carefulness. He seems in control of himself, thoughtful and able to develop plans to obain short- or long-term goals, and he is able to carry them out.

Freud listed a number of defense mechanisms the ego uses to control or defend itself against the id impulses and superego punishments. The principal ones are:

Repression. The ego applies psychic energy, itself derived from the id, to prevent the impulse or wish from reaching the conscious mind. The id, of course, applies energy in the opposite direction. There is an ebb and flow of power. In sleep, the impulses are gratified in the form of images. The power of the id impulse also grows in relation to the ego's repression under the influence of alcohol, narcotics, drugs and in cases of acute frustration, such as prolonged sexual abstinence.

Rationalization. The socially undesirable id impulse moves into the conscious mind, but the ego quickly changes its nature into something acceptable. If the impulse is an aggressively hostile one—to hurt a person by ridiculing him, for example—the ego protects itself from this knowledge, as well as from the punishment of the superego, by telling itself that this is only friendly kidding and thus quite acceptable behavior. The person who steals rationalizes that it is just a mistake, or that "everyone does it," or that he was just obtaining "his due." Lies are reduced to "misstatements," "errors," or harmless "white lies," or elevated to highminded efforts to "protect" the person being lied to.

Projection. The ego protects itself from recognizing an undesirable id impulse by attributing it to another person. Thus, a hostile, aggressive person accuses others of being hostile and agressive toward him. A woman repressing a strong desire for illicit sexual relations thinks men are wishing to molest her.

Introjection. In this case, the opposite of projection, the ego defends itself by identifying with another person. The hostile, aggressive man may fulfil his wish by identifying with and even "being" a gangster or movie villain. The woman desiring to be sexually molested may find relief from her impulses by identifying with a sexy actress in a film role.

Isolation of affect. This might be called incomplete repression. The person has a conscious memory of some unpleasant event in the past, but the emotion connected with it is repressed. The person remembers a serious automobile accident but not the emotional reaction he had to it.

Reaction formation. In simplest terms, the ego turns an undesirable impulse into its opposite. An aggressive impulse against one's parents might be kept unconscious by exaggerated feelings of love, tenderness and respect.

Denial of reality. This is most often seen in severe mental illness. Faced with overwhelming id impulses, the person separates himself from reality to enter a depressed state or fantasy world where the impulses cannot possibly be acted upon.

Sublimation. This is considered the most desirable of the defense mechanisms. Freud believed that all progress in civilization, arts and learning were a product of sublimation. The undesirable or destructive id impulse, along with its energy, can be turned into some desirable and constructive purpose by the ego, he thought. Sexual impulses are turned into painting, sculpture, music, and literature. Aggressive impulses are fuel for a doctor, lawyer, policeman, or builder. Indeed, one of the aims of psychoanalysis is to help the patient find constructive, sublimated uses for his psychic energy.

Freud used these theories to develop an explanation of mental illness. He saw aberrated conduct arising from *anxiety.* Anxiety may be said to be fear, but as Freud and most others use it, anxiety is a fear originating within a person's mind.

A person can have a fear based upon external events. He can be afraid of running across the street in traffic, of standing on a railroad track in front of a train, of putting his hand in a flame, of going to jail, of being punished by his parents, of flunking a grade in school, of being fired from a job, of having no money. These are legitimate fears based upon experience or knowledge that the results of such actions are likely to be unpleasant or painful.

An anxiety, on the other hand, is irrational. It is not based on knowledge or experience. Examples would be a person's fear that his parents will not love him, that he might find no friends, that his hair will fall out, that someone will attack him in the dark, that something awful will happen to him, that he has a fatal illness. It would be possible to think of circumstances in which each of these might be a realistic fear—an intruder is known to be in the house, or a person has physical pain —but in the absence of this, the fears are irrational. They are not based on knowledge. They stem from the mind of the person. They are anxieties.

In his later theories, Freud maintained some of his earlier ideas that psychoneuroses resulted from sexual maladjustments in early childhood. But he considerably expanded these ideas to include anxiety based upon concern with the ego and its failure to control the id and superego.

Freud distinguished three main types of anxiety, *real, neurotic* and *moral*. Real anxiety is similar to rational fears. It results from some legitimate danger in the external world.

Neurotic anxiety, according to Freud, originates in the id. The person fears that his id impulses will lead him to commit some undesirable or horrible act. Freud described three types of neurotic anxiety. In the *free-floating* variety, the person has a vague feeling of impending doom. He doesn't know what, but he is sure something will happen that is bad. He may temporarily decide that something specific will happen, but when it does not, he soon selects some other disaster to worry about. He is constantly nervous, agitated, fearful and apprehensive. Freud believed the person, although he does not realize it, is actually worried that his aggressive sexual impulses of the id will break through his ego controls.

A *phobic* anxiety derives from the same source as the free-floating type, but the fear is localized on a specific object or situation. A person can have a phobia of almost anything—high places, enclosed places, open spaces, blood, dogs, cats, horses, men with green ties, airplanes, cars, dancing, athletics, and so on. In each instance, the person can give a rational reason for the fear. People do fall off high buildings, horses kick or throw people off, insects carry germs, bleeding is unhealthy, dancing is no fun, planes crash, and so on. But such realistic dangers are rather slight in relation to the person's fear. Planes do crash, but the chances of a person's being in a fatal air crash are extremely remote.

According to Freud's theory, the phobias stem from id impulses which the person fears will break through. A person may be afraid of dancing because he unconsciously fears that his id impulse will lead him to sexually molest a girl. He fears snakes for the same reason, because the snake, in Freud's view, is a phallic symbol. He fears enclosed places because of a fear that his aggressive impulses may break through and cause him to attack someone. He fears other situations because he believes his death wish may cause him to harm himself.

With neurotic anxiety of the *panic* variety, the victim is—or feels that he is about to be—overwhelmed by his id impulses. He simply gives in to the impulses and engages in what therapists call "acting out" behavior. In mild form, he gets into a violent quarrel or fistfight with someone, tells off his boss, gets drunk, and becomes loud, abusive or profane. In extreme cases, he commits rape or robbery, hits someone with his car or, obtaining a gun, shoots a number of total strangers. All such actions result in punishment by society. He is ostracized by friends, physically hurt, fired from his job, or arrested and imprisoned. This means that external forces are now controlling the id impulses, a condition which the person usually greets with relief. The reaction to punishment is frequently calmness and acceptance.

Moral anxiety is similar to neurotic anxiety, but its roots lie in the superego rather than the id. If a person has consciously done or thought something that violates his conscience, the ego feels guilty, expecting punishment both from the external world and the superego. Anxiety results. In some cases, as with panic anxiety, the person may commit some act just to gain relief from his guilt feelings by earning some type of punishment. One of the characteristics of moral anxiety is that the more virtuous the person, the greater his capacity for guilt. A person with a strong conscience may feel guilty over some act, such as lying or boasting, that another person with less conscience would not give a passing thought to.

In all these types of anxiety, Freud believed, the person is never accurately aware of the real sources of his discomfort. He blames other people and situations for his fears and invents plausible reasons for being anxious. He simply does not realize or is unwilling to admit the existence of id and superego impulses that are the true causes.

Nor are such anxieties entirely bad. A well-adjusted person uses such anxieties both to protect himself from harm and to develop more appropriate ego defenses. Anxiety has led to the great civilizing works of man through sublimation. Through reaction formations, man has cultivated such qualities as kindness, helpfulness, self-sacrifice and love. Anxiety becomes a problem when the person is unable to control it acceptably or when he uses ego defenses in an exaggerated way that is socially unacceptable.

Freud felt that extreme forms of mental illness, the so-called psychoses, may be explained in terms of reactions to id impulses. Such gross symptoms of illness as deep depressions, manic bahavior, delusions, hallucinations and desires for aggressive actions toward others or oneself are ways to keep the id impulses from being carried out, if only because they are virtually certain to have the person put in protective custody in a mental hospital.

This has been a brief discussion of the main themes of Freudian analysis. None of the criticisms of Freud's theories and methods—and there are many—have been listed. There can be no complete understanding of Freud's work without knowledge of these criticisms. Some of these will come out in the next few chapters as we consider the Post- and Neo-Freudians, who disagreed with the master, broke away and founded other systems of psychoanalysis. Following them, there will be a critique of psychoanalysis and other insight therapies.

4

Alfred Adler:
The Individual Is Supreme

In 1902, Freud emerged from his years of secluded study to form the Wednesday Evening Discussion Group. It was composed of physicians and scholars interested in psychoanalysis and Freud's work. It later developed into the first psychoanalytic society.

Among the first Freud invited to join was a 32-year-old Viennese physician named Alfred Adler. He had come to Freud's attention both because of the nature of his work and because he had publicly defended Freud's theories and methods. Adler's membership was destined to be relatively short, for Adler broke with Freud in 1911 to found his own school of Individual Psychology. He was the first of Freud's close followers to break away.

Adler's importance in psychotherapy cannot be overstated. As the first dissenter, he set a pattern in his profession that has continued to this day, that is, the setting up of rival "schools" of psychotherapy by people disagreeing with Freud or with other systems of therapy. More importantly, Adler developed several original concepts both in theory and in methods. He offered a clear alternative to Freud that won widespread public acceptance, Adler being a brilliant speaker and writer, and he has had profound influence on other therapists. Adler's *Individual Psychology* is virtually defunct today, but his ideas live on in the theories and methods of large numbers of other therapists.

Adler, born in 1870, spent his early life in Vienna. He was a sickly child, with results that influenced his life's work. He had suffered from rickets as a child. This is a disease seldom seen today that is caused by a deficiency of calcium and Vitamin D. It leads to deformity of the bones. As a result, Adler could not walk until he was four years old. Shortly thereafter, he developed a severe case of pneumonia, which set him back again. When he was able to get around, he fell many times and had several accidents on the street. But Adler was determined to overcome these handicaps and become a doctor. He longed to join other boys in athletics, but since he could not, he immersed himself in his studies. Even his hobbies were of a botanical or biological nature, such as collecting pigeons and cultivating flowers. Ultimately Adler entered the medical school of the University of Vienna, which Freud had attended. He graduated in 1895.

In the medical school and the years that followed, Adler became a great favorite in Viennese coffeehouses. He was gregarious and full of good humor. Better, he was highly informed about psychology and philosophy and could quote generously from the classics. He also developed a strong social consciousness, ultimately becoming a Socialist. He deplored the appalling conditions in which the workers lived, many of whom became his patients. He was particularly struck with the high incidence of eye disease among tailors and studied the problem for a time. Soon he turned to neurology, hoping to combine both his medical background and his social interest to find some way to help the underprivileged.

It was only natural for Adler to join Freud's study group. He wanted not only to treat his patients medically but to help them socially as well. This meant helping them cope with mental problems, and Freud was offering a new approach to these matters.

Adler remained a medical man for some time after joining Freud. Drawing on his own childhood experiences, he studied the ability of body organs to compensate for structural weaknesses or injury. If a person has a defective heart valve, for example, muscles of the heart will enlarge to permit the flow of blood to be maintained. Similar situations develop with kidney malfunctions. Adler reported the case of a boy with a serious deficiency in vision from birth. When one of his eyes was damaged in an accident, the vision of the other eye noticeably improved. Adler published this work in 1907, promising to make the "connection" between clinical medicine and psychology at some future time. Freud was very pleased with Adler's work.

A year later, Adler began to do as he had promised. He proposed the possibility that the aggressive drive was the mechanism that enabled a person to overcome an organic defect through compensation. If there was a "confluence of drives," both aggressive and sexual ones, for example, the sexual drive would assume prominence over the aggressive. In that 1908 paper, Adler suggested that drives could be turned into opposites. For example, the instinct to be a voyeur (peeping tom) could be turned into exhibitionistic behavior. Freud later borrowed both these ideas, giving Adler due credit. He spoke of "confluence of drives" and termed a drive taking an opposite form the "reaction formation," which we have already encountered.

Adler's paper set the basis for the disagreement between the two men. Adler considered the aggressive drive the chief tool by which a person copes with the problems of living. Freud borrowed the aggressive drive and used it (Adler sarcastically said he had made a present of it to Freud), but buried it in his death instinct. He thought all drives had a power to become aggressive and saw no reason to give the aggressive drive special importance.

Personality differences also created friction between Freud and Adler. The younger man never had considered himself a disciple of Freud but saw himself, rather, as a junior colleague having a measure of equality and independence in his work. Adler apparently was miffed when Freud failed to invite him on his lecture tour of the United States in 1909. He felt that Freud showed favoritism toward Carl Jung, inviting him to the United States and also recommending him for president of the Second International Congress of Psychoanalysis in Nuremberg in 1910. Freud attempted to assuage these impressions that same year, naming Adler president of the Viennese Analytic Society and appointing him a coeditor of the group's professional publication.

Such measures were not early enough, however, for the theoretical disagreement between Freud and Adler was growing. In 1910, Adler first wrote about feelings of inferiority and laid the cornerstone for his theory of what was to become known popularly as the *inferiority complex*. He saw mental disorders, neuroses and psychoses as rooted not in biological instincts but in a person's strivings to overcome his feelings of inferiority.

Each person starts life with a burden of biological inferiority and feelings of inferiority stemming from his helplessness as a child surrounded by adults. Adler said that people react to the feelings of inferiority with "masculine protest," the cultural position of the man being one of strength, that of the woman one of weakness. He further proposed that every person carries within himself both the masculine and feminine attitudes. Life, then, is a struggle for dominance of the masculine over the feminine, strength over weakness.

Adler further proposed that sexuality is only symbolic. Women are neurotic not because of penis envy but because they envy the preeminence of men in our culture. To equal or dominate men they must relinquish their femininity, which they obviously cannot do. Neurotic disorders stem from this psychological struggle. According to Adler's theory, excessively masculine and aggressive men are not reacting to a fear of castration, as Freud proposed, but are overcompensating for their gross feelings of inadequacy as men.

In 1911, Adler went further—and too far for Freud. He said the Oedipal conflict was not related to the boy's desire to possess his mother sexually. Rather it was the boy's extravagant efforts to overcome his inferior status and to achieve superiority over the father and dominance over the mother. Adler also quarreled with Freud's theory of repression, seeing it as "only a small segment of the effects of the masculine protest."

A break between Freud and Adler was now inevitable. Adler was denouncing the central core of Freud's work, undermining his efforts of a lifetime. Freud said, "It is not a good thing for people who no longer understand one another and no longer agree to remain under the same roof together."

Adler accused Freud of insisting on conformity to basic doctrine and acting as a typically insecure, threatened eldest son. Feeling he no longer belonged to an open discussion group, Adler left the Viennese Psychoanalytic Society with nine other members in 1911 to organize the Society for Free Psychoanalysis. A year later the name was changed to the Society for Individual Psychology.

Over the years members of the two groups railed at each other, the Adlerians denouncing Freud as dictatorial and intolerant of ideas other than his own, the Freudians denouncing Adler as trying to usurp the role of his mentor. Both charges are probably incorrect. Freud worked for many years with associates who disagreed with him, giving them large measures of independence. Persons who worked closely with Adler saw nothing of the power-hungry person in him. It is probable the schism lay in the personalities of the two men and their widely divergent theories. The gulf between them was simply too large to be papered over.

The most unfortunate result of the schism was that the Adlerians, as the smaller group, took defensive stances. They tended to speak in broad, dogmatic generalities, such as "*All* neuroses are caused by . . ." and "*Every* neurosis can be explained by. . . ." There was little room in either Freud's or Adler's house for anything but the one true gospel as they saw it. It is a characteristic of the profession to this day.

Adler built an entire theory around the inferiority complex. Feelings of inferiority were the key to the human mind. "To be a human being," he wrote in *Social Interest: A Challenge to Mankind*, "means the possession of a feeling of inferiority that is constantly pressing on towards its own conquest."

The feeling of inferiority could result from a number of factors: an imperfect physique, physical deformities, defective bodily functions, deficient intellect, poor education, and a host of abrasive social relationships. He believed that the mere fact of childhood spent among powerful, demanding adults creates a feeling of inferiority in the best adjusted of youngsters and that the neglected, overindulged or hated child is absolutely certain to feel inferior. At a very young age the child works out a method, called his *life style*, which appears to him to be the most effective way to gain superiority, or at least minimize inferiority. This life style can be almost anything. The child can learn to be aggressive, destructive and a behavioral problem; shy and withdrawn; obedient, trustworthy and well-behaved; an achiever in school, sports, music, art or some other line of endeavor; or a deliberate underachiever, to avoid situations that might lead to failure.

Whatever the method, Adler wrote, "The goal of the personal purposive pattern is always the goal of social significance, the goal of the elevation of personal self-esteem, the goal of superiority. This goal is indicated by a variety of manifestations. It may be crystallized as the ideal either of useful achievement, of personal prestige, of the domination of others, of the defence against danger, or of sexual victories."

Adler saw character as the interlocking set of attitudes the individual had adopted early in life to cope most effectively with the inferiority-making situations of his life.

Three results of the strivings for superiority were proposed. One is *successful compensation*, leading to healthy adjustment to society, work and sex, the three challenges of life. A second is *overcompensation*, in which the efforts become exaggerated and lead to maladjustment. Examples are the small man who becomes cocky and aggressive, the weakling who becomes a gangster, the "sexpot" actress who insists that she be admired for her brains, the shy person who becomes a back-slapping extrovert.

The third result is a retreat into mental illness. Adler held that neurotic or psychotic illness is nothing more than an attempt by an individual, who is unable to attain his goal of superiority by legitimate means, to use symptoms of mental illness as an excuse to avoid situations in which he might fail, or as a means of emotional blackmail of friends and relatives to gain superiority. Neuroses and other forms of mental disturbance are, then, rather consciously planned by the person. This, as we shall see, is a view commonly held by learning therapists.

Adler believed that what Freud saw as repressed sexual material in the unconscious was neither repressed or terribly sexual. He believed the Oedipal complex was "quite consciously" used by people who fear failure in sexual relations. He believed homosexuality was similarly motivated and that frigidity in a woman (sexual indifference or an inability to have orgasm) is simply an attempt by her to humiliate her partner and gain a sense of superiority over him.

Neurotic behavior can be understood, Adler asserted, as a result of a person's establishing fictional goals for himself. Where a well-adjusted person will set realistic goals, the neurotic person establishes unrealistic or "fictive" goals that are impossible to reach. A built-in excuse for failure and his neurotic symptoms is thus created. The learning therapists have again borrowed from Adler when they maintain that the "ill" person doesn't want to get better.

Adler broadened this concept of fictional goals to include whole societies. He gave as an example the slogan "all men are created equal." He maintained that it and many similar statements are not true. They are unrealistic, impossible of attainment and probably undesirable, yet they have influenced the lives of countless people. The neurotic strives for superiority in pursuit of fictive goals, thus deepening his anxiety and worsening his social relationships. As we shall see, these ideas were borrowed by several schools of psychotherapy.

Adler saw war as a product of man's self-centered striving for egoistic gain. Peace would come, he said, only when man surrendered his self-centeredness and the search for significance and superiority in favor of the pursuit of work, love for his fellow man, and fulfillment of his social and community obligations.

Man's "will to power" must give way to good will toward his fellow man. He believed that children should be guided by parents and teachers toward this end. In 1919, he opened the world's first child-guidance clinic in Vienna. Until his death in 1937, he widely lectured to parents, teachers and guidance counselors in pursuit of these goals.

Adler also departed from Freud in his psychoanalytical method. He saw his role as therapist as that of a teacher, again predating the learning therapists. He felt it was crucial that there be no inequality between himself and the patient. Therefore, Freud's technique of sitting impassively behind the couch was not effective. Because he downgraded the importance of the unconscious, Adler was not interested in having the patient freely associate.

He sat facing the patient and engaged in free discussion. Adler saw his task as assisting the patient to understand the self-defeating nature of his life style and helping him develop a more productive method to cope with his feelings of inferiority. He thus felt the therapist should offer the patient interest, warmth and advice. They could discuss those experiences in the patient's childhood that had led to inferiority feelings. Dreams were analyzed as evidence of the patient's attitude toward something in the present.

Adler felt it was the job of the therapist to help guide the patient to establish social interests, but he cautioned against the therapist's doing it in any specific way. Adler never urged a particular conduct on a patient, such as becoming religious, joining a political party or having specific social relationships. He felt that the patient would do these things himself after having a positive experience with the therapist. Again, this idea has been used by a number of other therapies.

It is passing strange that Adlerian psychology is all but nonexistent today. For his work had tremendous influence on teaching, child guidance, religious counseling and all other aspects of work with people. Many other therapies use Adler's ideas. In a way, his theories were more useful than Freud's, for he was the first to view man as a member of a social and cultural environment and to emphasize its importance in his life.

5

Four Other
Disciples Leave Freud

The defection of *Carl Gustav Jung* in 1913 probably hurt Freud more than the loss of Adler. Jung had
contributed much to the psychoanalytic movement and
Freud had termed him his "crown prince."

Jung was born in Kesswil, a small Swiss village, in
1875. He was the son of a Protestant clergyman who was
greatly interested in Oriental and classical studies. As an
only child till age nine, Jung was shy and lonely. His
father taught him Latin from the age of six and he became a bookworm, immersing himself in reading, particularly of the classics.

He enrolled in the University of Basel in Switzerland
in 1895, intending to study anthropology and Egyp-
tology, but he soon switched to natural science, and
finally to medicine. Just before graduation he read a textbook on psychiatry and instantly knew his life's work. In
1900 he went to work at an important mental hospital
and university psychiatric clinic in Zurich. His teacher

there was Eugene Bleuler, an important psychiatrist of the era who had been associated with Freud.

Jung did serious work during the next several years, earning an international reputation as a psychiatrist. He had long been interested in spiritualism and seances. His first book sought to explain the occult in psychological terms. He did extensive research in word associations as a means of identifying unconscious problems and wrote a well-received book on the subject. The word-association method is still widely used in psychology today. A series of words are spoken to a person, who is instructed to say the first word that comes into his head. The word "mother" might provoke a reply of "warmth," "love" or "child." The associative words are a mixture of ones expected to cause emotional reactions, such as "fear" or "sex," and neutral words such as "sky" or "tree."

By judging the patient's replies, the length of time it takes him to reply on emotional words, the words to which he cannot reply and his reactions to various words, the psychiatrist is able to pinpoint problem areas in the subconscious, or so Jung believed. Jung called the combination of an idea and a strong reaction to it a "complex," thus introducing it into the psychological language.

Jung's most important work was studying *schizophrenia*, or *dementia praecox* as it was called in those days. The nature of his studies is too complex to detail here, but suffice it to say that he believed mental disease was caused by a chemical toxin or poison and that the substance could be produced by psychological means. Mental upsets caused production of the toxin, which in turn caused schizophrenia.

In all these early writings, Jung praised Freud, quoted from his writings and said that Freud deserved wider recognition for his original theories. In 1906 Jung began a correspondence with Freud, and then, near the end of 1907, he journeyed to Vienna to meet the great man. Their first meeting lasted thirteen uninterrupted hours. Freud was highly impressed with Jung, calling his a "truly original mind." He saw him as "the Joshua destined to explore the promised land of psychiatry," which Freud, like Moses, was only permitted to view from afar.

Jung's presence had important advantages for Freud's movement. He was the first non-Jew to become involved. As Freud later wrote, "It was only his (Jung's) emergence on the scene that has removed from psychoanalysis the danger of becoming a Jewish national affair." He was also non-Austrian. Freud and nearly all his coterie were Viennese, and Vienna simply did not count for much in scientific circles. But Switzerland did. Jung's arrival, particularly since he had a reputation in his own right, gave status and an international thrust to psychoanalysis.

Toward this end, Jung founded the Freud Society in Zurich and organized the First International Psychoanalytical Congress in Salzburg in 1908. A journal was begun, with Bleuler and Freud as directors and Jung as editor. In 1901, Jung gave up his post as chief physician at the Zurich mental hospital to devote himself full time to psychoanalytic activities. The following year a Congress was held at Nuremberg and the International Psychoanalytic Association was founded. Jung was elected President over the angry protests of the Viennese segment. But Freud was pleased. He considered Jung talented, loyal, independent and energetic.

All was not sweetness and light, however. Freud and Jung harbored ambivalent feelings toward each other. The periods of collaboration and good feelings were studded with times of doubt and suspicion. More than once, Freud seems to have had fears that Jung wished to dethrone him as the leader of the psychoanalytic movement and take his place. There was an instance of this in 1909, when both men were in Bremen, Germany. Jung wanted to see some relics of anthropological interest. Freud became annoyed and concluded that Jung's interest in dead bodies indicated a wish for Freud's death.

For his part, Jung seemed to have great difficulty in making up his mind about Freud's theories. On some occasions he would embrace them wholeheartedly. On others, he expressed reservations or just omitted certain aspects of them. These omissions regularly dealt with sexual aspects of Freud's theories.

Before long, these incipient problems widened into an irreparable breach. In 1911, Jung had published *Wandlungen I.* It was an exhaustive analysis of ancient myths, legends, fables and stories from the classics in which Jung drew a parallel between the fantasies of the ancients and those of children. Jung concluded that everyone's mind naturally "possesses . . . historical strata" inherited from ancestral experience, which show up in a psychosis when there is a "strong" repression.

Freud was pleased with the work, for he always liked to see psychoanalytic writers delve into mythology. He had issued a statement agreeing with Jung that dreams and neurotic fantasies are similar to the thinking of a child and to the mentality of primitive peoples. However, in 1913, at the time of his break with Jung, Freud retracted that agreement, reducing Jung's theory to the level of a "parallel" or "analogy."

The real problem came with the publication of *Wandlungen II* in 1912. Jung gave a non-Freudian interpretation to the idea of the libido. Freud used the term to mean the sex drive or the drive for pleasurable gratification. Jung desexed the libido, giving it a meaning closer to "life force." Later, he went further. "The sexuality of the unconscious," he wrote, "is not what it seems to be; it is merely a symbol . . . a step forward to every goal of life, but expressed in the unreal sexual language of the unconscious and in the thought-form of an earlier stage; a resurrection . . . of earlier modes of adaptation."

Other events encouraged the break. Jung felt a loss of Freud's confidence in him. Freud became irritated with Jung because he was devoting too much time to research and not enough to activities of the psychoanalytic movement. In 1912, Jung "played down" Freud's sexual theories on a second lecture tour to America. He became tardy in answering Freud's letters, which angered the master. The correspondence became more impersonal and less frequent. In September, 1913, the two men met for the last time at the International Congress in Munich, where Jung was reelected president. The estrangement lasted a long time, for Freud died at age 83 in 1939 and Jung at age 84 in 1961. Their disaffection was peculiar, for, as many writers have pointed out, their differences seemed more in the realm of semantics (the meaning of words) than in substance.

Jung's contribution to psychoanalysis is hard to describe, because much of his writing is difficult, entering the realm of metaphysics. He was also the least scientific of the major figures in the profession. He had an unscientific habit of attempting to describe something partly known in terms of something wholly unknown.

In addition to the term "complex," he gave psychology the words *introvert* and *extrovert*. In a paper read at the Munich conference in 1913, he described two psychological types, the introverted person, who withdraws his general interest (libido) from the world and turns it inward, and the extroverted, who has an intense interest in the outside world. Most psychologists consider that theory interesting but not terribly valuable. Hardly anyone is wholly introverted or extroverted. Most people are a combination of the two.

Jung's major thesis was that below each individual's unconscious mind, which contains the repressed memories from the person's own experience, lies a *collective unconscious*. This consists of ancestral memories passed on from prehistoric ages and from man's evolution from a primitive animal state through his early struggles for survival and his socialization. Jung maintained that we carry in our bodies and minds traces of the experiences of cave men and subsequent steps in the development of man and his civilization.

He believed that every person is predominantly introverted or extroverted in his conscious mind. The unconscious mind, though, is a mirror image of the conscious; that is, reversed. The outgoing, extroverted person is introverted in his unconscious mind, and vice versa. The masculine-acting man has a feminine unconscious.

Jung divided man's lifetime development into three physico-mental stages. The presexual period lasts from ages three to five and is concerned with nutrition and growth. The prepubertal period marks the beginning of sexuality. The time of maturity lasts the rest of a person's life. Jung believed the Oedipal conflict is founded in love for the food-providing mother and becomes tinged with sexuality only in the prepubertal phase. The castration complex was seen by as a symbolic sacrifice of infantile wishes and has nothing to do with sex.

Jung felt that neurotic anxiety is a result of the unequal development of the personality. Like Adler, Jung had little interest in the past history of the patient. His concern was with the present. "I ask what is the necessary task which the patient will not accomplish," he wrote. In analysis, Jung sought to put the patient into contact with his healing collective unconscious, believing that it offered the wisdom of the ages to the patient. He often sought to indoctrinate the patient, frequently encouraging religious feelings.

Today Jung is highly regarded by clergymen and theologians. Although his theories and methods are little used by practicing psychotherapists, many of his ideas have influence.

William Stekel was another of Freud's disciples who departed the fold. Born in 1868 (he died in 1940), he was a brilliant analyst and a prolific writer who has had considerable influence, much of it unrecognized. That influence is more in the area of methods than of theory.

Stekel emphasized the role of the therapist in the curative process. He came to dislike Freud's passive role in analysis, as well as what he considered Freud's use of the patient to advance his own knowledge and theory. Stekel felt that the first task of the therapist was to cure the patient. He was prepared to take a most active role to achieve this goal. He did not wait for important information about the patient to appear through free association. He intuitively deduced the problems from analysis of the patient's dreams and his general attitudes and actions. Using this intuitive insight, he actively attacked the patient's thinking, not hesitating to offer advice and even exhort the patient to change.

Like Adler, Stekel was not interested in the patient's past history. He prefered to work with material from the present, and, again like Adler, he concentrated on fictive (unrealistic) goals. A characteristic statement was, "Day after day I attack the patient's system by storm, showing that he can get well betwixt night and morning if only he will discard his fictive aims." He had the Adlerian view that the patient's "resistance" to improvement was not unconscious opposition to the emergence of forbidden wishes, but a defense against the treatment itself. Being cured means the acceptance of adult responsibilities, and the patient wants to avoid these.

Stekel's "active analytic psychotherapy," as he called it, rarely took more than six months. Stekel felt the time was shortened because he actively sought to demolish the patient's illusions and childish use of emotion.

Many other schools of therapy have borrowed from Stekel. Even those who admit to a Stekelian approach seldom follow him rigidly but borrow also other methods. Many do not stick to the six-month course of treatment, nor are they as aggressively active as Stekel was.

Sandor Ferenczi (1873–1933), a Hungarian, never did break with Freud and remained one of his most trusted friends until his death. But their relationship became strained at times largely because of Ferenczi's use of different techniques of analysis. Ferenczi's concern, which many others have to this day, was to find a way to shorten the time needed for analysis. Freud had his patients come an hour a day five days a week for one, two —perhaps five or more years. This rather limits the effectiveness of analysis, for very few people can afford either the time or money for such protracted treatment.

Ferenczi first acted on a suggestion of Freud's that analysis should be carried out in a state of privation. Ferenczi urged his patients to avoid sexual relations, to take as little time as possible for urination and defecation, and not to eat or drink for pleasure. He believed that if the libido could be denied natural expression in these ways, more of its energy would go into expression of repressed feelings.

The result of the privation was predictable. The patients became angry toward Ferenczi, pouring out their resentment, frustration and aggressive feelings. At first Ferenczi believed this reaction had excellent therapeutic value. But soon he realized the hostility was entirely a result of the patients' present difficulties and not related to childhood experiences in any way.

In 1927, he abandoned the privation technique and adopted its opposite, offering the patients love and permissiveness. He considered neurotics to be people who had never been properly loved and accepted as children by their parents. What such people need, he reasoned, was a substitute parent who will offer them as adults the warm, loving, permissive atmosphere they were denied as children.

Ferenczi carried acceptance just as much to extremes as he had privation. He permissively accepted, and indeed encouraged, patients to act out childhood grievances. He would treat patients as young children, talking to them in the appropriate manner, even playing childhood games with them. He was even known to take a patient on his lap to help him dramatize some childhood incident.

Too, he engaged in the definitely un-Freudian activity of revealing himself to the patient. He would admit his mistakes and shortcomings in an effort to prove that not all parents are self-righteous, intolerant, unloving figures.

Such techniques are so thoroughly un-Freudian that it is difficult to see how a total break was avoided. The answer probably is that Ferenczi accepted Freud's theories wholeheartedly and made no attempt to develop his own theory.

The defection of *Otto Rank* (1884–1939) must have been another blow to Freud comparable to the loss of Jung, for Rank, like Jung, had been designated heir apparent to lead the movement after the founder's death.

Rank had been most unhappy during his teenage years in Vienna. He suffered from rheumatism and was intensely lonely. He was estranged from his mother and would not speak to his alcoholic father. His diary contains this passage: "I grew up left to myself, without friends, without books. I feel for most people no sympathy. I wish not to be buried, but to be burned. As a grave marker, I would like a rough, unpolished block of stone." Rank considered suicide at various times. Instead, he coped with the loneliness and emptiness by developing his creative talents.

Freud first met Rank when he was enrolled in a technical school and was supporting himself in a machine shop. Freud was impressed with Rank's knowledge. He helped him with his emotional problems and offered him financial support while Rank completed his doctorate at the University of Vienna.

Rank joined the Viennese Psychoanalytic Society at Freud's invitation in 1906. For the next two decades he was a highly regarded member, acting as secretary of the society, co-editor of its journal, and as founder and director of the Psychoanalytic Institute of Vienna. Particularly after the defection of Jung, he was the resident expert on myths, legends and cultural matters. He was admired for his "vast erudition" and ability to interpret dreams.

But Rank, wishing to express his own creativity and longing for greatness, began to have thoughts of his own. He joined Ferenczi in seeking ways to shorten analysis. In 1923, they suggested that a time limit be set on analysis.

The following year brought Rank's book *The Trauma of Birth*. In this, he elaborated on a statement made earlier by Freud that at the time of birth a baby is overwhelmed with stimulation of the senses. Rank stated that the individual forever seeks to return to the blissfulnesss of the mother's womb. The healthy child, through later experiences of separation from the mother (weaning, for example), is able to discharge his anxiety. Mental illness, in Rank's view, results both from the wish to return to the womb and from fear of it because of the painful experiences at birth.

Rank believed that sexual intercourse was a symbolic returning to the womb. He suggested that a young boy does not refuse to recognize the existence of female genitals because she has no penis (Freud's castration complex), but because of the horrible experience of birth. He theorized that the homosexual is so frightened of the female organs that he cannot enjoy normal love. The Oedipal conflict, Rank thought, is simply an effort of the boy to rid himself of his fear of his mother's genital region.

Freud was initially ecstatic over this work. He called it "the most important progress since the discovery of psychoanalysis." The Central Committee of the Viennese Society was not so impressed, however. It felt that Rank had made too radical a departure from Freudian theory and persuaded Freud to admonish Rank for reducing all of psychoanalysis to one theme and one that completely disregarded the role of the father.

The criticism put Rank in a state of turmoil, for he could not break with Freud at that time. He had several analytic sessions with Freud and recanted his book, blaming it on "unconscious conflicts." Since Freud had "personally forgiven" him, he hoped to do better in the future. By 1929, however, Rank was able to break away. He ceased to apologize for his work and no longer wrote in Freudian language.

About this time, Rank also began to separate himself from his birth trauma idea. In 1930 he admitted he had carried the idea to absurd lengths. Instead, he began to analyze disorders in terms of important periods in a person's life in which he breaks away from parental influences and expresses his individuality.

Still later, Rank developed the concepts of will and counter will. He denied that the individual is ruled by the instinctive id and remorseless superego, as Freud suggested. He felt that individual has a will, "a positive guiding organization and integration of self which utilizes creatively, as well as inhibits and controls, the instinctual drives." The counter will is directed against parental restrictions. The two develop until the individual has gained independence and becomes truly creative.

Rank felt that the normal person both expresses his individuality and conforms to the wills of others. The neurotic either exaggeratedly conforms to the wills of others or excessively rebels against them. He saw the role of the therapist as helping the neurotic, through transference, to become a creative person.

Like Adler and others, Rank was more interested in the present than in past problems. He liked to set a time limit on therapy, and he liked to keep the therapy flexible so as to adapt to the individual needs of the patient. He believed the relationship between the patient and the therapist should be unique and creative. He felt that the patient, not the therapist, should control the choice of methods that would best solve his problems. As we shall see, these ideas and methods would have great influence on later therapists.

6

The Neo-Freudians—
Horney, Fromm, Sullivan

The dissent that began with Adler and continued with Jung, Stekel, Ferenczi and Rank accelerated. More and more theories and methods developed, each departing from Freud in small or large ways. Today's psychiatrist or analyst has a variety of methods and ideas with which to work. Analysts are rather secretive about their therapeutic techniques, but it is believed that few of them still practice analysis as Freud did. For this reason, the word "classic" is usually attached to Freud's method, much as the word is used in music or literature. One studies Shakespeare or Mozart, but he does not attempt to write or compose as they did.

Of particular importance in the development of analysis were (or in some cases are) the so-called Neo-Freudians, principally Karen Horney, Erich Fromm and Harry Stack Sullivan. Trained as Freudians, they broke away to form new theories and methods, yet their ideas are rooted in Freudian concepts. They accept or are indebted to some of Freud's concepts while departing in others. All have two aspects in common. First, all seek to cure neuroses by offering the patient *insight* into his unconscious motivations; and second, all emphasize cultural influences over Freud's biological instincts. The term *dynamic culturists* is often applied to them.

Karen Horney (1885–1952) was born in Germany and graduated from the University of Berlin in 1913 with a medical degree. Shortly thereafter she became associated with the Berlin Psychoanalytic Institute (as was Fromm) and for fifteen years was an orthodox Freudian analyst. She came to the United States in 1932, becoming, in turn, associate director of the Chicago Institute and lecturer at the New School for Social Research in New York. But it was as a staff member of the New York Psychoanalytic Institute that she began to stress her original theories. In 1941 she founded and became dean of the American Institute for Analysis, where she remained until her death. She was a powerful writer. Her books, *New Ways in Psychoanalysis, Our Inner Conflicts, Self-Analysis*, and *Neurosis and Human Growth*, were widely read in the 1940s and 1950s. Like Adler, she wrote more for the lay public than for members of her profession. She therefore had far greater influence on public thinking than on other analysts.

Two aspects of Horney's work are important here, her criticism of Freud and her own theories. In professional circles, her criticisms are highly regarded by many who do not agree with the theories she substituted. She thought herself only as "correcting" Freud, not replacing him. She felt that he was a prisoner of nineteenth century thought and morals and thereby needed to be modernized, particularly in the light of anthropological studies of primitive, non-Western cultures. She always felt that coming to America gave her the courage to develop her own theories. She found America to have a culture different from that of Europe, offering "greater freedom from dogmatic beliefs."

Horney made four main criticisms of Freud's theory. First, she said, his theories have a biological orientation, which is apparent in his instinct theories, his emphasis on hereditary factors, and his tendency to explain psychological differences between the sexes in terms of anatomical differences. He assumed the oral, anal, phallic and genital phases, as well as the Oedipal problems, to be innate and biological in origin. Environmental and cultural factors were of little importance to Freud as compared with man's innate fear of castration and woman's belief that she had already been castrated.

Second, Freud assumed that "human nature is the same the whole world over," as Horney expressed it, whereas studies of people like Margaret Mead have shown there are societies where aggressiveness, for example, is not innate. Horney felt that Freud, ignorant of such research, failed to consider the effects of culture and environment on psychological formation.

Third, Freud engaged in dualistic thinking, again characteristic of the last century. He saw psychic factors in pairs of opposites, life and death, conscious and unconscious, ego and id, masculinity and feminity. He further conceived of these opposite pairs as physical systems. Energy spent in one system, in his view, is automatically lost to its opposite. Love of others impairs self-love, masculinity robs feminity, and so on.

Fourth, Freud was "mechanistic-evolutionistic" in his outlook. This led to his assumption that present manifestations not only are conditioned by past events, as in

Darwin's theory, but contain *only* the past. An example of such thinking would be that water turned into steam is still water. Another point of view would say the steam now has different properties and is governed by different physical laws. The mechanistic-evolutionistic mode of thinking led Freud to assume that adult attitudes are *nothing but* a repetition of childhood experiences or attitudes, that nothing much happens to a person after age five, that he is a prisoner of the birth trauma or Oedipal conflict or oral or anal pleasures, repeating them over and over throughout his life.

She felt that Freud, as a prisoner of nineteenth century thought, was led into some traps of reasoning. He became unduly pessimistic about human nature, causing him to maintain, as she put it, that "not only the striving for power, but every kind of self-assertion is [to be] interpreted as an aim-inhibited expression of sadism. Any kind of affection becomes an aim-inhibited expression of libidinal desires. Any kind of submissive attitude towards others becomes suspect of being an expression of a latent passive homosexuality." A child loves his mother because of his libidinous desires. Possessed of death instinct, he seeks to destroy others to save himself. Horney felt this was patently untrue. Other cultures do not have these drives. They are not innate in all men. And how did man, if he possesses these innate aggressive drives, ever form social groups in the first place?

She also criticized Freud for assuming that his libido theory would explain all psychological trends— a mistake not dissimilar to Adler's use of inferiority complex or Rank's development of the birth trauma. Horney said that Freud, in expounding the theory of the libido, was trying to understand a whole machine by examining a wheel. She felt that emphasis on sexual drives to the exclusion of all else misrepresents a patient's views of human relationships, the nature of neurotic conflicts and the role of cultural factors. It leads the analyst, she believed, into assuming a limitation on the effectiveness of therapy (the patient being unable to alter his biological makeup) when in fact no such limitation exists.

Finally, Horney criticized Freud, as many others have done, for his heads-I-win-tails-you-lose type of reasoning. The boy who loves his mother, according to Freud, has an Oedipal conflict. The one who does not is repressing his desires or engaging in a reaction-formation. If a man is mean and nasty to others, he is showing aggressive feelings. If he is kindly and friendly, he is having a reaction formation. If he thinks a person is hostile toward him, he is projecting. If he thinks the person is kind, he is repressing homosexuality. In short, such reasoning can explain all things after the fact but predict nothing before the fact.

As others had done, Horney took issue with Freud's explanation of the Oedipal conflict. She did not believe that conflict is universal or that it is caused by innate biological factors. She felt it can have two causes. First, the parents wittingly or unwittingly stimulate the child sexually. Second, feeling insecure, unloved by his parents, the child clings to one of them in hopes of receiving reassuring affection. This may look like an Oedipal complex, but it is not.

The criticism most frequently made of Karen Horney is that in developing her own theory of neurosis she fell into the same trap that ensnared Freud, Adler, Rank and others. In trying to negate Freud's emphasis on biological factors, she bent over backwards to emphasize social and cultural factors. Biological instincts have little or no place in her thinking.

Horney began her theory by denying the universality of normal behavior. What may be normal in one culture is abnormal in another. Nonetheless, all neurotics have two traits in common. They are rigid in their reactions and there is descrepancy between their potential and their accomplishments. Where a normal person will approach different situations in different ways—that is, is flexible—the neurotic tends to approach all human relationships in a predetermined manner. A normal person may be frustrated when he seeks to accomplish something, but the frustration is usually caused by external forces. A man may lose his girl to another fellow, fail to achieve a promotion because of his own lack of education or experience or because of the superior ability of a competitor, or fail in business because of economic conditions. The neurotic, on the other hand, fails because of something within himself that precludes accomplishments.

Horney thought there was more than one type of neurosis. A normal person can have a *situational neurosis* when the external situation he faces is full of conflicts. An example might be the case of the woman who wants to care for an invalid mother, while wishing also to marry and begin a life of her own. Wars frequently create "battle neuroses" because of the conflicts involving love and hate, saving lives and killing.

The true neurosis is a *character neurosis*, Horney believed. External forces may aggravate certain personality defects in a person, but the defects were there long before the situation developed. The war veteran who turns sadistic and criminal had such tendencies before going into battle. All character neuroses are based upon disturbances of character that originated in childhood and resulted in what Horney called *basic anxiety*.

This she described as a feeling of being "small, insignificant, helpless, endangered, in a world that is out to abuse, cheat, attack, humiliate, betray, envy." Such feelings are caused by the absence of genuine warmth and affection from parents during childhood. The parents were, of course, reacting to their own neuroses. She felt that unconditional love is essential for a child's normal development. Without it, the child comes to look upon the world as "unreliable, mendacious, unappreciative, unfair, unjust, begrudging and merciless." She continued:

> ... the child not only fears punishment or desertion because of forbidden drives, but he feels the environment as a menace to his entire development and to his most legitimate wishes and strivings. He feels in danger of his individuality being obliterated, his freedom taken away, his happiness prevented. In contrast to the fear of castration, this fear is not fantasy, but is well founded in reality. In an environment in which the basic anxiety develops, the child's free use of energies is thwarted, his self-esteem and self-reliance are undermined, fear is instilled by intimidation and isolation, his expansiveness is warped through brutality or over-protective "love."

In a word the child is *insecure*. The world is frightening and dangerous. He should not assert himself. Loneliness is a way of life. He grows up wishing to be protected and to be taken care of, to put all responsibility upon others, yet he is suspicious of others and cannot trust them.

To cope with such feelings, the neurotic takes defensive action. Horney suggested that the neurotic has ten basic needs, causing him to search for affection and approval, for a person to take over and run his life, for restriction of life within narrow confines, for power, for exploitation of others, for prestige, for personal admiration, for personal achievement, for self-sufficiency and independence, and for perfection and unassailability.

Of these she felt four were paramount. The neurotic need for affection drives the person to seek affection and approval that can never be satisfied. It is not possible for another person to love him enough. He is frequently promiscuous, seeking the unobtainable in still another bed. And, never having had love and always seeking it, he can never return love. He fears emotional dependency, yet, he demands unconditional love regardless of how unloving his actions toward the other person may be. It is a case of love me no matter what I do.

Horney's neurotic drive for power is similar to Adler's inferiority complex. The neurotic is driven to be superior in all things and to dominate all others, the origin of such feelings being the person's fear, anxiety and feelings of inferiority. He is driven to be right all the time, to have his own way. He envies the abilities and superiorities of others and feels the need to disparage, frustrate and defeat them. Yet he is constantly fearful of retaliation, leaving him in a state of turmoil.

The neurotic need for withdrawal leads the person to seek self-sufficiency so that he will not be emotionally dependent upon anyone.

The neurotic need for submission causes the person to be nearly totally dependent and unassertive. He allows himself to be used and abused, accepts the opinions of all others, particularly if they denigrate himself, and avoids all independent thought and action.

Later, Horney summarized all these defense mechanisms into three: moving *toward*, moving *against* or moving *away from* people. In the first he tries to win affection and lean on other people. In the second he assumes their hostility and decides to fight them. In the third he simply tries to avoid people. In short, he reacts with helplessness, hostility or isolation.

Such tactics might work, except that life does not permit it. A helpless person is forced to stand on his own two feet once in a while. A hostile person must seek the help or cooperation of others from time to time. And the isolated individual must come into intimate contact with some people some of the time. When this occurs the individual experiences *basic conflict*. He does not know how to act and he approaches the new situation in the same manner as all other situations. If predominantly helpless, he is plunged into anxiety when stood up for a date and reacts with anger and increased demands. The person who usually reacts with hostility and becomes ill, for example, will continue to berate the doctor who comes to save his life. Such attitudes may work for a time, but eventually new situations arise and the neurotic finds himself searching for new remedies. He is inmeshed in an ever-widening circle of conflicts.

To cope with this enlarged situation, the neurotic assumes a "second line of defense." He "eclipses" the problem by taking on a reaction opposite to his former one. This is akin to Freud's reaction formation. The hostile person becomes affection-seeking, the helpless person hostile. Or, he isolates himself, indicating this is an effective defense for helpless and hostile neurotics. Or, he creates an "idealized image" of himself. Or, he externalizes his problem, blaming it on others or the external world. He is not at fault.

The *idealized self* is important in Horney's theory. It is similar to Freud's superego and Adler's fictive goals. She felt the idealized self, a godlike creature of perfection, is bound inevitably to hate the neurotic's *actual self*, that most imperfect of creatures. The aim of therapy is to help the patient discard the idealized self and its whole collection of neurotic needs so as to face the actual self, understand basic anxieties and conflicts and learn new ways of achieving the goals of love and inner security. In this way the person's *real self* can be released toward free, healthy development of the personality and the person's potential.

In therapy she tended to be more directive and active than classical Freudians. She felt the patient must go through a "disillusioning process" before the idealized self could be abandoned. The various neurotic needs, defenses, strategems and conflicts should be pointed out to the patient before new, more constructive self-images and methods could be developed.

Erich Fromm was also born (1900) and educated in Germany, lecturing at the Psychiatric Institute in Frankfurt and the University of Frankfurt. He, Karen Horney and Harry Stack Sullivan met in Berlin to discuss their various theories. Fromm came to the United States in 1934. He has taught at Bennington College, the National University of Mexico, Michigan State and New York Universities. He has lectured widely, conducted an analytic practice and written many books, including *Escape from Freedom, Man for Himself, Psychoanalysis and Religion, The Sane Society,* and *The Art of Loving.* His books are widely read by the general public and he has had wide influence both on the public and the profession. Yet, Fromm has never sought to develop a separate system of therapy.

Trained in Freudian analysis, Fromm does not hesitate either to draw upon Freud's concepts with which he agrees or to criticize those he dislikes.

Fromm points out that Freud believed there was a basic division between man and society and that human nature is at its core evil. Man is antisocial and it is the function of society to domesticate him. Man may have some expression of his biological drives, but ordinarily the instincts must be thwarted. Only by sublimating his sexual drives has man been able to develop culture and civilization. It is Freud's assumption that the less man satisfies his instinctive drives, the more civilization he achieves. Less suppression of instincts leads to less neurosis, but also less civilization.

Fromm disagrees with Freud's biological orientation and maintains that the fundamental problem of psychology has nothing to do with the satisfaction or frustration of any instinct but is rather that of the specific kind of relatedness of the individual toward his world. In Fromm's opinion, the relationship between man and society is constantly changing and is not fixed as Freud believed.

Fromm agrees each person has basic instinctual drives or needs, such as hunger, thirst, and sex. These are common to all men. But having the needs is one thing; fulfilling them is another. The time, method and manner by which a man satisfies his hunger, thirst and sexual needs is determined by his society or his culture. That hungry men give away their last piece of bread, that people sacrifice their lives for a cause, cannot be explained biologically. Only in terms of a man's society and culture can it be understood. The problem of psychology is to determine how the individual relates himself to society, the world and himself. This skill is not innate. It is acquired or learned through the environment.

Through the process of evolution man has become unique, a "freak of the universe," Fromm believes. He described man as:

> . . .a part of nature, subject to her physical laws and unable to change them, yet he transcends the rest of nature. He is set apart while being a part; he is homeless, yet chained to the home he shares with all creatures. Cast into this world at an accidental place and time, he is forced out of it, again accidentally. Being aware of himself, he realizes his power-lessness, and the limitations of his existence. He visualizes his own end; death. Never is he free from the dichotomy of his existence; he cannot rid himself of his mind, even if he would want to; he cannot rid himself of his body as long as he is alive—and his body makes him want to be alive.

Fromm traces human history in terms of the develop-ment of individuality. Man began as a part of nature, only dimly aware of his existence as a human being. He existed in a state of "cosmic unity" with both his fellow man and the physical universe around him. This relieved him of loneliness, yet it bound him to nature and his social group and blocked development of his individual-ity.

By the Middle Ages, man had lost his sense of unity with nature, but he still possessed social solidarity. The social order was fixed and the individual was tied to his role in the society to which he had been born. Indeed, he was tied to the land. His dress identified his class and occupation. His rules of conduct and economic life were rigidly controlled by the Church, which offered comfort, solace and the love of God. The man of the Middle Ages may not have been free and individual, but he was not alone or forgotten.

This began to change with the Renaissance, which was basically an expression of individuality in the arts and science. Commerce grew and with it capitalism. A man was now able to rise or fall by his own efforts. The individual was recognizable by his wealth, dress and accomplishments. The Protestant religion intensified this individuality. Man stood alone, naked before God. Man was told to accept the basic evilness of his nature and to submit to the will of God. These factors combined to give man greater freedom and individuality, but at the cost of a terrible feeling of aloneness and, for many, helplessness. Fromm sees man's problem as an effort to escape these feelings of aloneness and helplessness so as to return to a state of oneness with nature and other men.

Fromm describes methods by which man tries to relate to society to ease his feelings of loneliness and helplessness. In *moral masochism* the individual feels the need to be dependent and to rely on others in a weak and helpless manner. In *sadism*, the individual seeks to make others dependent upon him, to exploit them or to make them suffer. *Destructiveness* seeks to eliminate any possible threat or comparison by destroying it. In *automaton conformity* the person attempts to wipe out any differences between himself and others and thus wipe out loneliness and helplessness. Fromm believes this is the reason so many people submit to totalitarian regimes.

He further describes five character types:

1. The receptive character believes that everything he wishes must come from an outside source. He is dependent and wants to be taken care of.
2. The exploitative character tries to satisfy his desires by

force, cunning and exploiting others. He would
rather steal than produce by his own efforts.

3. The hoarding character keeps what he has and ignores
   what he did not produce himself. He is orderly,
   punctual and tends to withdraw from the world.

4. The marketing character has a tendency to adapt him
   self or sell himself to others.

The productive character is the normal person capable
of love for others and demonstrating ". . . man's
ability to use his powers and to realize the potentialities inherent in him."

Fromm believes that neuroses stem from man's struggle to relieve the loneliness, helplessness and powerless-
ness which modern industrial society forces upon him.
Innate biological needs, while they exist, have little to do
with these problems. Man will best solve them by developing his capacity to love other human beings, while
making use of his own creativity and individuality.

Harry Stack Sullivan was a native American psychiatrist, born in Norwich, New York, in 1892. He obtained
a medical degree at the Chicago College of Medicine and
Surgery in 1917. He is important in psychotherapy because, more than any other insight therapist, he sought
to create an entirely new system independent of Freud.
Since he emphasized social factors rather than the biological, he is the leading theorist among the social psychologists. Unfortunately Sullivan died in 1949 at a
rather young age. He did not have time to present his
theories in a body of literature. What is known has been
compiled from various scientific papers he wrote. Unfortunately, these are rather difficult reading, for he had a

tendency to invent new words or to give different-from-usual meanings to existing words (neologisms).

Sullivan believed that all "human performances" may be classified either as the pursuit of satisfactions or the pursuit of security. Satisfactions he related to the bodily needs for food, drink, sex, sleep and so forth. He saw no great difficulty in satisfying these needs, except in the case of sex. Security was used by Sullivan to refer to ". . .all those movements, actions, speech, thought, reveries and so on which pertain more to the culture which has been embedded in a particular individual than to the organization of his tissues and glands." He felt that man has much more difficulty satisfying these needs and that anxiety and mental problems are rooted in this difficulty.

The person comes to evaluate himself in one of three ways, as a "good me," "bad me," and "not me." The "good me" attitude leads to feelings of security, or euphoria, or self-satisfaction. The "bad me" leads to anxiety states. The "not me" is a primitive state of loathing, dread or horror primarily seen in severe mental cases.

The origins of such feelings may lie very early in childhood. Sullivan believed a mother passes anxiety on to her child, perhaps very soon after birth, through a process he called "empathy." If the mother is anxious or upset when she feeds the child, the infant realizes or feels this, although he hardly understands it. This is accomplished through a process of "emotional contagion or communion." If she is relaxed, happy and secure, the child also shares such feelings through empathy. In this manner, as well as through consciously expressed parental attitudes, the child develops a view of himself as either good or bad.

To this background is added the child's experience

with tension. An unsatisfied need, such as hunger, will lead to tension, both in the involuntary muscles of the stomach and in the voluntary muscles of the legs, arms and torso. The infant reacts to the discomfort of these tensions by crying. Satisfaction of hunger releases the tension and frequently leads to sleep. Something similar happens in the case of the child's psychological needs for security. Experiences in having these needs satisfied join our empathetic reaction to parental attitudes to create either the good me or bad me or a combination of the two. In effect, the child grows up in a combined state of euphoria and anxiety, relaxation and tension, comfort and discomfort.

Such attitudes, stemming unavoidably from childhood, are greatly affected by interpersonal relationships with friends, teachers, neighbors and others. These relationships modify the person's attitudes toward himself, for better or for worse. His view of himself may be improved because other people think well of him, or the reverse may occur. But more is involved. The person may develop an idealized view of other people. These, Sullivan termed "parataxic distortions." One of the prime purposes of his therapy was to eliminate these distortions so that people and situations can be viewed realistically.

Sullivan agreed that there is an unconscious, which manifests itself in dreams, fantasies, errors and accidents, but his view of it was unlike Freud's. He viewed the mind much as the headlights of a car shine into darkness. The headlights reveal a small amount of the darkness just ahead—the conscious mind. More of the darkness can be illuminated by turning the lights in a different direction. This is Freud's "preconscious"— material not in the conscious mind but easily recalled into it if needed. But beyond the headlights, even if they are moved in all possible directions, lies a great mass of darkness, the unconscious. Sullivan thought the unconscious unimportant to the task at hand, the objective of getting the individual where he wanted to go. He equated the unconscious with unawareness. It is unnecessary to problem solving, he believed, although it causes a certain amount of anxiety or uneasiness.

Sullivan believed that the person develops early in life a means of coping with his situation which he holds on to quite desperately. If he has a good feeling about himself, he strives to maintain it, remaining unaware of anything (from the unconscious) that might lead to anxiety. At all costs the self will endeavor to maintain its original form and direction. This is true even if the view of the self is bad, hateful or derogatory. He suggested that this "bad me" will "inhibit any disassociated feeling or experience of friendliness toward others; and it will misinterpret any gestures of friendliness from others. The direction and characteristics given to the self in infancy and childhood are maintained year after year at an extraordinary cost, so that most people in this culture—and presumably in any other—because of inadequate and unfortunate experiences in early life, become 'inferior caricatures of what they might have been.' " He felt that both love and hate, aggression and submission, as well as all states in between, could be explained by the need to avoid anxiety about the unknown and to win parental love and affection.

Sullivan typed people according to their prevalent attitudes toward other people. The ten most common types are the nonintegrative or psychopathic personality who seems to lack any strong social feelings; the self-absorbed, who engages in fantasy; the incorrigible, who is hostile to all but those he regards as inferiors; the negativistic, who have given up hope of obtaining love and settle for attention; the stammerer; the ambition-ridden personality; the asocial or detached, lonely people; the inadequate or clinging-vine type; the homosexual; and the chronic adolescent who pursues but never finds the ideal in life.

In therapy, Sullivan tried to find the methods the patient had learned in childhood to avoid anxiety, which thus caused him difficulties in interpersonal relationships in later life. Then he sought to attack these directly to break them down. After he revealed the distortions in interpersonal relationships, the ideal result, he believed, should be changed attitudes on the part of the patient toward himself and other people.

7

Non-Freudian Insight Therapies

It was perhaps logical and certainly inevitable that the deviations of Adler, Jung, Horney, Fromm and Sullivan should lead to heresy, the total or near-total denial of Freud and his theories and methods. Each differs from the others and from Freud, but all have one thing in common: they seek to cure mental maladies by giving the patient insight into his problems.

The best-known, most significant and most controversial of the non-Freudian insight therapists is *Carl Rogers*, who was born in Oak Park, Illinois, in 1902. He studied theology at the Union Theological Seminary in New York and progressive educational philosophy as well as clinical psychology at Columbia University. He has taught at Ohio State University and at the Universities of Chicago and Wisconsin. It may be said that his theory and methods are not only typically American in outlook, but *Midwestern* American.

105

Rogers' system is the antithesis of Freud's. It is called *client-centered* or *nondirective* therapy. The therapist seemingly does very little but offer the patient *unconditional positive regard*, that is, constant, genuinely felt approval and acceptance as a person, including all his ideas and actions. Rogers believes the worst of men possesses innate forces driving him toward personal growth and fulfillment. When the patient is accepted and approved of, his fear is removed, permitting the innate forces to cure him. At no time does the Rogerian therapist express disapproval, lecture, instruct, threaten, advise or even offer an opinion. The patient does it all himself.

An even greater heresy in psychiatric circles is Rogers' stated belief that no particular education or training is necessary to be a client-centered therapist. Any warm-hearted, interested person can do it, he maintains, if he adheres to a few simple rules. Indeed, it is often a disadvantage for the therapist to be so knowledgeable that he is cast into the role of an "expert" who tells the patient what to do.

Rogers first developed the method of treatment, then later superimposed a theory to explain it. The theory, while largely non-Freudian, bears many similaritites to Horney, Sullivan and others.

Every person, Rogers theorized, develops a self-concept or self-structure. It is a way of viewing himself based on his physical makeup, his experiences in life, and the views others have of him. The latter are usually distorted by the person. His self-image—which seems quite similar to Horney's idealized self—is developed rather early in life. Thereafter the person either accepts the information that enhances the self-concept or rejects that which does not, eliminating it from awareness. A Freudian might say that the undesirable information is repressed into the unconscious, but Rogers denies the existence of the unconscious, or at least maintains that it has no importance.

Rogers abhors any attempts by the therapist to diagnose or classify a person as schizophrenic or suffering from any particular ailment. In his terminology, the unproductive, self-defeating or unhappy person perceives any experience out of line with the self-concept as a threat. Inevitably, he leads a self-limiting, circumscribed existence marked by rigidity of thoughts and action. Rogers feels that the person who does something others consider destructive or defeating is only doing so out of a mistaken belief that such actions create self-esteem. Rogers believes that if that person can be surrounded by an atmosphere totally free of any threat to his superstructure, he will work out more productive and satisfying social relationships.

The conclusion is inescapable that Rogers' theory is rather simplistic and shallowly imposed upon his method. It seems to borrow heavily from Adler, Horney, Freud and others. It is his method of therapy that is innovative and important.

Rogers believes that the therapist must work only in the present. Since the person coming for therapy is apt to have a strongly negative view of himself—his actions being hardly likely to live up to his self-image—the task of the therapist is to offer highly positive approval and acceptance. He never criticizes the client. Nor does he disapprove or suggest alternatives. The therapist tries as hard as he can to understand what the patient has done and his reasons for doing it. He tries to put himself in the place of the client. His comments are largely limited to reviewing the patient's situation and experience so that he, the therapist, is certain to understand exactly what the patient reports. In short, the therapist and the patient are trying to communicate so that there is no misunderstanding.

The therapist's attitude must not be an intellectual exercise. He must sincerely feel in an emotional way that the client is a worthy individual—a likeable, even lovable individual, with whom the therapist sympathizes and towards whom he has not one shred of negative attitude. This is unconditional positive regard.

From time to time, the therapist will explain the nature of their relationship; that is, that the patient is going to cure himself and that the therapist is not going to do it for him. If it seems useful and not upsetting to the patient, a question and answer procedure may be engaged in so the therapist can draw out additional information from the client. Never does the therapist offer any interpretation. Similarly, the therapist does not impart any insight into the client's difficulties. He wants the person to achieve insight, of course, but the client must do it without any prompting from the therapist. Absolutely everything is up to the client. If he is to be cured, he will do it himself.

Rogers began to use this method in the late 1940s and early 1950s. He had a high success rate. Large numbers of clients were cured and the time for cure was relatively short. But in those days Rogers was rather selective in the patients he accepted. Most were people with relatively mild disorders, vaguely unhappy and underachievers.

Later, Rogers began to expand his treatment to difficult cases of mental illness, homosexuality and similar conditions. He made no predictions as to the effectiveness of his method, but he felt that the nature of his therapy was such that no harm would come to the person if the treatment was ineffective. In treating difficult mental states, the Rogerian method has tended to produce less statistically impressive results. But that is an achievement, not a criticism. The classical Freudians tend to accept mild problems, avoiding the hard-case mental patient who is resistant to nearly all efforts to change him.

Rogerian methods have been broadly accepted in the United States, particularly among clergymen, guidance and marriage counselors, teachers, lay advisors, sociologists, and social workers. His belief that expertise is detrimental has attracted many laymen to his method.

More than any other insight therapists, Rogers and his followers have thrown open their methods to public knowledge and scientific scrutiny. Through tape recordings, films and similar techniques, they have shown scientists and the public exactly what they do in therapy. They have tried to apply scientific methods of measurement and evaluation. They do not claim to have the end-all, be-all of psychotherapy but believe their methods are useful in a variety of cases. This attitude of humility and scientific inquiry is unique among the insight therapists.

Another "insight" method is that of *Albert Ellis*, a New York City psychologist trained as a Freudian. The lack of success of the methods he had been taught forced Ellis to create a new system, which is, perhaps, a transition between the insight therapists and the learning therapists. It is difficult to classify him in either school.

Rational Therapy, as Ellis calls his system, is rooted in the fact that man is a verbal animal. His thoughts, beliefs, and attitudes are expressed through speech. Even when he is reading and writing and is not speaking, man unconsciously translates the written word into mental, unuttered sounds so that measurable vibrations are set up in his vocal cords. Ellis believes, therefore, that the way to control thought is through speech.

He believes there is great need for people to control their thoughts. Consciously or unconsciously, large numbers of people believe or think statements that are untrue either wholly or in part. If the statement were held up to rational examination, it would be rejected as untrue or unreasonable. Ellis believes that people carry around such thoughts in the form of internalized sentences, which they repeat over and over to themselves. If these sentences are negative thoughts about the person himself, they can seriously affect his self-esteem and his actions and relationships with other people.

A simple example of Ellis' internalized sentences would be "I am a terrible person," said by a person who says and believes it. Now that is patently untrue. The speaker may have done some bad things. He may have some unlikable qualities, all of which are subject to change and self-improvement. But even if his negative qualities remain unchanged, he still has many likeable qualities and has done many good things. So how can he be a terrible person? There simply is no such thing as a terrible person.

Another simple example would be the sentence "Nobody likes me." Ellis would perhaps reply that such a statement is irrational. Some people he knows must have regard for him. And even if he is totally unliked in his present circle of acquaintances—itself highly unlikely— there is no reason to assume that enlarging his acquaintances would not lead to some friendships. Nor, is there any reason to assume that a present condition of unpopularity is permanent. Some changes in attitudes and conduct could quickly lead to improved social relationships.

There are a large number of irrational or illogical ideas which Ellis believes people tell themselves over and over. These in turn set limits on a person's view of himself and his relationships with the external world. Some others are: "It is absolutely necessary to be loved and approved by others"; "The attitudes of others toward me are more important than what I think"; "Since we live in a community, it is selfish to be self-sufficient, and therefore one should depend on other people"; "Everyone should help others"; "One should not do unpleasant things but should rebel against them because unpleasantness should be avoided."

In Ellis' view, none of these statements is patently either true or untrue, at least as an absolute. He argues that it is pleasant, but hardly necessary, to be loved and approved of; that postponement of present pleasures often leads to greater satisfactions in the future; that being self-reliant leads to self-respect and the respect of others.

A common Ellisian statement is, "You don't have to be perfect, and neither does anyone else." He uses it often, believing that many people constantly berate themselves for their imperfections, losing self-esteem over the slightest deviation from perfection, and get into social difficulties because they demand perfection from others. He is suggesting that it is only human to err. A person should strive for self-improvement, but in a more relaxed atmosphere, forgiving himself for mistakes and permitting others the same luxury.

Ellis is highly directive in his therapy in the sense that he is aggressive in attacking the patient's irrational assumptions. By attacking the illogical statements repeatedly, he hopes to undermine the patient's belief in them and lead him to accept more viable statements. He is not directive in the sense of imposing a life style on the patient. He does not try to inculcate a new set of values. He only wants to make the person's values, whatever they are, rational and liveable.

A similar theory is that of *E. Lakin Phillips.* He is a psychologist who believes that people live by assertions that are self-defeating or simply don't work. He looks upon the patient as having made assertions about himself and others that are incorrect and have small chance of working. Such an assertion might be "People are no good. They are out to harm me." If an individual lived by this idea he would be extraordinarily suspicious. He would be inhibited in nearly every social relationship. He would be unliked, thereby intensifying his own gross social difficulties. This in turn leads to a vicious circle that Phillips calls *redundant behavior.* Unliked, he is more suspicious (or whatever). His life becomes a round of discomfort and futility.

In therapy, Phillips attempts to attack these assertions, undermine the logic behind them, demonstrate their repetitive and self-defeating nature and lead the person to more useful assertions.

Even more non-Freudian than Rogers, Ellis and Phillips is *Andrew Salter.* It is difficult to classify him. The insight therapists call him a learning therapist, but the latter reject him as too superficial. Because he seeks to have the patient achieve a small level of insight, perhaps he does belong in that group.

Salter seeks to have patients liberate their feelings. He agrees that society imposes some limitations on a person's freedom to express himself, but he believes most people carry around a view of these limitations that is much more stringent than it needs to be. He seeks, urges, even commands patients to express their feelings, to act in a normal, healthy way without concern for social consequences.

Toward this end, he urges patients to say whatever comes into their minds without fear of social repercussions; to register feelings through facial expressions and gestures; to be argumentative, attacking the views of other people with whom they disagree, not worrying about social reactions; to talk about themselves as much as they please; to accept and enjoy praise whenever they can get it; and to live an unplanned life, doing or saying whatever comes into their heads, unmindful of the reactions of others.

Salter admits this sort of conduct can be carried too far and get a person into difficulty. An uninhibited urge to take off one's clothes and stroll down the street could cause a variety of difficulties, including legal ones. But Salter maintains that his therapy, if used within reason, is far better than the narrow, restricted lives most neurotics lead. He maintains that only by releasing inhibitions and being oneself can the person learn to live a freer, more sensible life.

A wide variety of other techniques are used, including hypnosis, group therapy, painting and theatricals as methods of self-expression, communal bathing in the nude as a sort of "laying on of hands," to reach people by touching them. There are perhaps as many methods of psychotherapy as there are people to practice them. Indeed, an individual therapist may treat each individual patient in a different way, seeking those methods that seem most likely to be effective with him. But this leads us into a critique of insight therapy.

8

A Critique
of Insight Therapies

An attempt to evaluate Freudian and other insight therapies must begin with the observation that few men in history have had as much influence on Western thought and mores as Sigmund Freud.

Perhaps the entire fabric of our lives has been altered by his theories. Because of him we have irrevocably changed our way of looking at ourselves and our bodies; our attitudes towards our drives, instincts, and "glands"; our comprehension of personality-developing forces in early childhood, and thus our methods of child rearing; education; work; literature, art and music; counseling of all varieties; medicine; treatment of mental illness; social relationships; our attitudes towards other people and our understanding of the actions of others; relations with minority groups and even between nations. The world has today, because of Freud, a greater awareness of basic human motivations and how these are or could be expressed.

114

Freudian therapy is basic today. It is taught, either positively or negatively, in probably every school or institution that trains people to work with the mentally disturbed. No member of these professions is considered properly trained if he lacks a comprehensive knowledge of Freudian teachings. Until very recently nearly every worker in these fields was trained as a Freudian. If some later departed from Freud in search of other methods, they were certainly greatly influenced by the man from Vienna.

All this adds up to tremendous influence for one man. Perhaps no other field of study in modern times has been so dominated by the work of a single individual.

Therein lies the root of criticisms that have been made of Freud and the Freudians. In large measure even today —and wholly until the last few years—Freud's precepts were accepted as gospel by his followers. Any deviation, any criticism, was denounced. Freudians used Freud's theories to denounce the deviant or critic. As the case might be, he suffered from repressed Oedipal feelings because he denounced Freud, the father figure; he projected; he had reaction formations; he suffered from latent sexuality of one variety or another because he objected to the sexual theories of Freud; and so on. There was, in short, a high level of religiosity to Freudian thinking. Freud's followers looked upon his teachings as a pious person views the Holy Bible. They came from God and could not be explained or disagreed with. His word was truth. The sincere therapist who found himself obliged to make certain criticisms of Freudian therapy was beyond the pale and forced to be an "outsider" in his chosen profession. As we have seen, large numbers of people elected to be outsiders.

The most damaging criticism of all insight therapies—

a criticism that has never been refuted despite many attempts to do so—is that it does not work. In the late 1950s, British psychiatrist *H. J. Eysenck* made what might be called a study of studies. He evaluated the published reports of virtually all therapists of whatever persuasion to determine their effectiveness. How many patients had the therapists reported treating and how many of those were improved or cured of their maladies? He did not question the findings reported by the therapists. He simply compiled and reported them. Because of the controversial nature of Eysenck's findings, he repeated the study again in the 1960s with similar results.

To put his report simply, if three people with mental problems do *not* enter therapeutic treatment, two will get well, presumably as a result of their own thinking, of coping with their own problems, of a change in their situations, or of help from their family and friends. Eysenck found, on the other hand, that if three people with mental problems enter therapy for treatment, two of them will get well. Therefore, *treatment by psychotherapy is about as effective as no treatment at all*, the only difference being the amount of time and money invested in treatment. And the money is significant, for therapists charge from $25 to $100 an hour for their services. The only exception to this finding, Eysenck noted, was among the learning therapists, who report that 80 to 100 percent of their clients are improved by their methods.

Eysenck's studies have been upsetting to insight therapists. Arnold A. Rogow, in *The Psychiatrists*, quoted a therapist who found Eysenck's findings "disconcerting." In responding to Rogow's questionnaire, the unnamed psychiatrist said, "Many of my patients tell me they feel better. I don't know what that means. Does it mean they feel better because they saw me rather than a minister, or that in spite of seeing me they feel better?"

Another psychiatrist described by Rogow went on an extended trip abroad, arranging for his patients to call another psychiatrist if they had difficulties. Returning after several months, he discovered that only two of his patients had called his colleague. There was no change in the proportion of his patients who felt improved, became worse or stayed the same. The psychiatrist added that he was "shook up but good" to discover that his patients did just as well or as poorly when he was absent as when he was present.

Yet insight therapists are not charlatans. They honestly believe that they are helping patients and can cite cases of patients they have helped. Psychiatrist Jerome Frank has endeavored to postulate some reasons why patients may be improved in therapy, reasons that have little to do with the actual curative actions of the therapists.

The patient may see the therapist as a man of expertise who will cause him to improve. Believing in the therapist and having new hope for the future, he begins to think and act more constructively. Since the patient has to spend significant sums of money for the treatment, thus depriving his family, he feels obliged to improve from the therapy, and his family, having spent all the money, acts differently towards him, thus changing his life situation. The therapist may have given the patient some assignment of some kind, such as making friends or applying himself regularly to his work. These may change the patient's behavior and help him realize that he is not helpless. Finally, the patient may be so desperate for any kind of assistance that he is benefited and improved.

Insight therapists have offered various reasons for their failure to achieve results better than no treatment at all. These may be summarized as follows: first, the patient was deficient, not ready for therapy and not motivated to benefit from it. Second, the therapist did effective work but was undermined by the patient's family or the hostile society in which he lived. Third, the therapist was effective, but too many other therapists are incompetent, bringing the average down.

It may be said that none of these are valid arguments. In their treatment of physical diseases, which psychiatrists try to emulate, doctors can usually cure the condition even if the patient does not wish to be cured, or they can motivate the patient to want to get well. If the environment is important to the patient's recovery in psychiatric cases, then it is the task of therapy to prepare him to live in that environment or to change it. If there are incompetent therapists, then it is the task of the profession to determine what competence is and how it may be achieved. Doctors in physical medicine do exactly this, as do many other professions.

It is a most serious charge to make that insight therapy is no more effective than no treatment at all. Almost as serious is the charge that Freudian and other forms of insight therapies are grossly unscientific. Parts of Freud's theory have been in existence for three-quarters of a century and all of it for half a century, yet in that time very little of it has been either proved or disproved on a scientific basis.

Indeed, it is generally conceded that there is no possible way to set up a scientific study to gather evidence either in support of or in refutation of Freud's hypotheses. Consider the unconscious. In Freud's view, it is both unknown and unknowable. It's alleged content is repressed. Even when unconscious material reaches consciousness, as is alleged to be the case in dreams, it is in altered, symbolic form. The services of an analyst are needed to interpret the dreams, and every dream is subject to several interpretations. Therefore it is impossible to set up a scientific experiment to determine if the unconscious exists and, if it does, what is in it.

Consider the Oedipal complex, a cornerstone of Freud's entire theory. It is said to be an unconscious process occurring in three-to five-year-old children. The child does not know he has an Oedipal conflict, and all such knowledge is kept from him by various processes such as repression, sublimation, reaction formation and projection. Again, the conflict, being unconscious, is unknowable and not subject to scientific inquiry. The gulf between Freudian assertion and science widens because of the heads-I-win-tails-you-lose logic of Freudians. If loving one's mother is evidence of an Oedipal conflict and so is not loving one's mother, then there is no possible way to accumulate evidence in support of or in denial of Freud's statement.

About all that can be done is to make the observation that nearly all toddlers of three-to-five years, both male and female, seem to have a great deal of affection for their mothers. The Freudians take this observation and erect the Oedipal edifice from it. But other evidence and other interpretations are available. Adopted babies have the same fondness for the women who are not their natural mothers. Babies reared by nurses and governesses have been known to show more affection for them than for

their mothers. Lower forms of animals have the same
parent-child affection, even in those animals where the
father does not participate in the raising of the offspring
and may, in fact, be unknown. Mother-child affection in
humans can be interpreted as a desire of the child for
warmth and softness, for security, for regard for the
person who offers food and comfort, and in several other
terms.

A similar line of inquiry can be used against all of
Freud's postulates, as well as Adler's inferiority complex, Jung's collective unconscious, Rank's birth trauma,
Horney's idealized image, Sullivan's dissociation,
Rogers' unconditional positive regard, and Ellis's irrational statements. All are basically unprovable, and in
the absence of statistical evidence of their effectiveness
they are extremely unscientific. Belief in an idea as an
article of faith does not substitute for factual evidence.

A further charge is made that modern psychiatry has
theories not far removed from those of ancient
demonology. The Oedipal conflict, for example, is no
more provable or unprovable than the primitive idea
that the deranged person had been seized by an evil
spirit. Too, there seems to be more than a little in common between evil spirits and evil instincts, id impulses,
an irrational superego, unconscious lusts and repressed
aggressive tendencies. Worse, it may be said that modern
electric shock treatment, with drug-induced convulsions, as well as drugs which leave the patient so tran-
quilized as to be dull and uninteresting, are not entirely
removed from medieval tortures.

All such criticisms of insight therapies may be summarized as a quarrel with the medical model. Psychiatrist
Thomas Szasz and a number of learning therapists
whom we are about to meet view the concept of mental

and emotional disorders as "illnesses" to be a bankrupt one. The medical model, after a century, is not supported by much scientific evidence, nor has it shown itself to be very effective. Enter the learning model.

9

Behavior is Learned

Most people think of learning as that which occurs in school, the acquisition of information and concepts. But this is only part of learning, for people also learn behaviors. We learn to avoid dangers, to elicit a desired response from people, to act in such ways as to obtain happiness or eliminate unhappiness. Learning therapists believe that we have learned a vast number of things, even though we do not think of them as learned and have little or no idea how we learned them. They further submit that we learn to be crazy, self-defeating, unproductive and unhappy. They insist that either such behaviors, which insight therapists call neuroses or psychoses, can be unlearned or new, improved behaviors can be learned as substitutes.

These beliefs are rooted in what is called *learning theory*. From exhaustive experiments with rats, cats, dogs, chickens, monkeys and other animals, as well as with humans, psychologists have developed a body of evidence of how animals and man act in certain situations, how they both learn and unlearn, what type of behavior results from various forms of learning, and why both the learning and the behaviors occur.

Thus, learning theory is a large area of psychological study. It is applied to education, job training, advertising, politics and many other fields. It is also being used in psychotherapy. Much of the important work has been done by men who have no particular interest in treating the mentally deranged. A notable example is Harvard Professor B. F. Skinner. He has never developed a system of psychotherapy, but many others have applied Skinner's laboratory findings to human behavior with often startling results.

It is not possible here to present a comprehensive review of learning theory. The effort here will be to describe briefly those elements of learning theory which are most often applied to behavioral disorders.

Two general comments about learning theory are in order. First, researchers in learning theory endeavor to apply rigorous scientific discipline to their work. They try to set up careful experiments, removing as many extraneous factors as possible, make accurate observations and measurements as factual results, and then interpret those results in specific, nongeneral terms. Second, many of the major elements of learning theory seem oversimple. A common reaction is to say, "I knew that all along," or, "It's common sense." Psychologists, however, reply that people didn't know it all along but only thought they knew it, that many of the seemingly simple findings have subtle effects people do not realize, and that many of the discoveries actually violate "common sense."

Russian psychologist *Ivan Pavlov* has much the same

relationship to learning theory as Freud has to analysis. Pavlov (1849–1936) was a contemporary of Freud and did his most important work about the same time as the Viennese doctor. Pavlov also lived to old age and saw his work recognized the world over and himself celebrated. Many others have added to Pavlov's work. The term "classical" is now ascribed to Pavlov's work as it is to Freud's.

Pavlov's most celebrated discovery was the *conditioned reflex.* He worked with dogs, which ordinarily salivate at the sight or smell of meat. Shortly before the food was placed before Pavlov's test dog, a bell was sounded. After a number of trials, the dog began to salivate at the sound of the bell, even though no food appeared.

Pavlov did many other experiments. In one a dog was shocked on his foreleg following a tone. The shock made the dog lift his paw. Soon the dog was lifting the paw at the sound of a tone when no shock was forthcoming.

Such seemingly simple experiments were psychological bombshells at the turn of the century. They were powerful evidence that rigorously scientific experiments could be set up which offered at least a chance of understanding animal and human learning methods and behavior. Many others began similar experiments. Pavlov's experiment also demonstrated that a dog, at least (and perhaps man also), can learn to do illogical things. It doesn't make much sense, from a dog's point of view, to salivate at the sound of a bell or to lift his foreleg when he hears a tone. Moreover, Pavlov's experiments suggested that learning occurs whether the subject wants to learn or not. The dog was hardly enthusiastic about learning to salivate at the sound of a bell. This, too, would have important repercussions in psychotherapy.

If we take Pavlov's experiment, we can learn a little

necessary learning theory terminology rather quickly and painlessly. Learning theorists state that every form of behavior, or *response*, is a result of a *stimulus* (plural: *stimuli*). An obvious example would be placing your hand on a hot stove. The heat is the stimulus and the response is jerking the hand off. In Pavlov's experiment, the food was the stimulus and salivating was the response. But, because the dog has no control over these, the food is *unconditioned stimuli* and the salivating is *unconditioned response*. When the dog was taught to react to the sound of the bell, he received a *conditioned stimulus* and made a *conditioned response*.

In Pavlov's experiment, the dog salivated (responded) not just to one tone or bell but to several closely related tones. In psychological terminology, this is *generalization*. People also do this, and usually to a much greater extent. If you learn that placing your hand on a hot stove results in pain, you generalize this learning so that thereafter you do not stick your hand in fireplaces, under lighted matches, or above Bunsen burners, and you do not walk into burning buildings unless you are trained as a fireman. You give appropriate regard, not just to flame, but to electric heaters. In short, you avoid hot things.

There is abundant evidence that all learning is generalized. To give another example, if you had an unpleasant experience with a teacher, particularly when you were quite young, there is a risk that you might generalize this learning to include all teachers, even though some might be very pleasant people, or indeed to all schools, and even to education itself.

Pavlov's dog did not stay permanently trained to salivate at the sound of a tone. After a few trials, he ceased to salivate when the tone no longer produced food. In human terms, the dog "forgot" that the bell signaled the arrival of food. In learning theory jargon, this process is called *extinction*. This is a rather complex process in learning to which we will return in a moment, but in simple terms, for purposes of explanation, let's try to illustrate. Suppose you had a job for which you were paid every Friday. Unknown to you, your employer went out of business. You would put in your full week's work with the expectation of payment on Friday. When you were not paid on Friday, what would you do? You might quit, saying you weren't going to work without payment. You might work a second week. If payment was not forthcoming then, you surely would quit.

Or, if a man asked a girl for a date and she consistently refused, giving him no encouragement at all, he would stop asking her out. Both cases would have engaged in extinction learning. When a behavior or action does not result in any sort of reward, punishment or *reinforcement*, it is abandoned. Extinction occurs.

Pavlov's work was transferred to America by celebrated psychologist *John B. Watson*, whose school of therapy was called "behaviorism." It was highly popular in the 1920s and 1930s but is considerably less so today. Other learning therapists consider it an oversimplification, labeling it the "muscle twitch" method of therapy.

But Watson did a great deal of work that was influential in the development of psychotherapy based on learning principles. One example was the case of Albert, the baby son of a woman employed at the same hospital with Watson. Watson observed that Albert, aged nine months, was remarkably placid, reacting with smiles and coos to almost any situation that might produce fear. He showed no evidence of fear, for example, when presented with a white rat, rabbit, dog or similar animals.

With associate Rosalie Rayner, Watson began an experiment to create what would be called a phobia in Albert. Watson observed that the baby was startled and frightened if a loud sound was produced by hammering a large steel bar behind his head when Albert's attention was directed elsewhere. He reacted with whimpering, crying and similar behavior indicative of fear.

In the experiment, a white rat was offered to Albert. As he reached out for the animal, the gong was sounded. Albert appeared startled, but did not cry. In the second trial, the gong was sounded just as Albert touched the rat. He startled and whimpered. After eight trials Albert began to cry at the mere sight of the rat. And, Watson showed, Albert generalized his fear. He also reacted with fear to a rabbit, a fur coat, cotton wool and a Santa Claus mask.

Unfortunately, Albert was taken from the hospital environment before Watson had a chance to attempt to cure Albert's phobia, leaving one strange individual who was afraid of animals, fur and Santa Claus. Watson commented sardonically about the interpretations Freudian analysts might make in years to come, if they attempted to cure Albert's phobia without knowing its cause.

The experiment was completed a few years later by Watson's co-worker, Mary Cover Jones. She found Peter, age 3, who seemed to be Albert a few years older. He was afraid of rabbits, a rat, a fur rug, fur coat and a feathered hat. No one knew what had caused these fears, but afraid he was. Miss Jones attempted to *recondition* Peter. In her first effort, Peter was brought into the lab with three other children, none of whom were afraid of a rabbit. When the animal was introduced into the lab, Peter progressed from a great exhibition of fear to indifference and finally to following the example of the other children and patting the rabbit. He said happily, "I touched him on the end."

At this point Peter became ill from scarlet fever and was gone from the experiment for two months. Shortly before his return, he had a frightening experience with a large dog. When he was tested again, all his original fear of the rabbit had returned. Reconditioning was resumed, but by a different method. Peter was placed in a high chair and given food. The rabbit was brought into the lab in a cage and brought as close to Peter as was possible without the child's exhibiting fear. At each succeeding trial the rabbit was brought a little closer. Eventually, Peter was petting and holding the rabbit and became quite fond of it. Testing showed that he also lost his fear of furs, feathers and similar objects.

The experiment is important for several reasons. It showed that it is possible to retrain or recondition a person even though the cause of the learned behavior is unknown. Further, even though the first effort at reconditioning was undone by a bad experience with a dog, it was quite possible to recondition the subject a second time. What is learned can be unlearned and relearned a number of times. The experiment also showed that social pressures—the other children in the lab in this case—aid reconditioning, and that learning is generalized to include similar objects.

The work of Pavlov and Watson was important, but that of American psychologist *Edward Lee Thorndike* (1874–1949) made far greater impact on the development of learning therapies. Thorndike's most famous experiment was with a cat, which he placed in a cage which the animal could open only by pulling a string. Omitting some complicating elements in the experiment, it suffices to say that as the cat engaged in some random behaviors, crying, scratching, clawing, and pushing, it pulled the string, apparently quite by accident, and escaped from the cage. After a number of trials, the cat unerringly pulled the string whenever he was placed in the cage.

Psychologists call this *instrumental learning.* In simple English it may be translated as problem solving. The cat learned to solve the problem of getting out of the cage. This is the type of learning most often used by people. We learn that certain behaviors either produce a desired result or avoid an undesired one.

Thorndike did many experiments with animals and proposed what is known as his *Law of Effect.* In simplest terms, Thorndike stated that if an act results in a desirable state of affairs, it is more likely to be repeated. If the act is followed by an undesirable state, it is less likely to be repeated.

Thorndike's law seems ultrasimple. One might term it common sense. But there is an element of some subtlety to it. The law states that you would be more apt to repeat an act that is followed by a desirable condition, but it does not mean that the act itself caused the desirable condition. This is of some importance, for it offers an explanation of how some people learn seemingly illogical behavior.

To illustrate this point, suppose you wore a brown sweater to the school basketball game and the team won. Perhaps the following week you again by chance wore a brown sweater with a similar result. Suppose at this point you observed, or a friend pointed out, that the team won each time you wore the brown sweater. You deliberately wear the brown sweater to all the games and the team continues to win. Logically, your attire had nothing to do with the victories. But illogical or no, you see a desirable result from the act.

If you put your mind to it, you could think of many similar cases of learned illogical behaviors, including people who always have the same food for breakfast or lunch, sit in a particular seat, or follow a certain route to work or school. With a little more effort, it is possible to see how rigid, neurotic behaviors might result from such a learning process.

Vast research into instrumental learning has been conducted over the years by large numbers of people. One important branch of this study deals with *avoidance* or *escape learning.* A famous experiment was conducted by O. Hobart Mowrer and Neal Miller. A rat was put into a specially constructed cage. One side of the cage was separated from the other by a low wall that a rat could jump over. On one side, the floor could slide away to reveal a grid which administered an electric shock. On the other side, the floor was normal, administering no shock.

In the experiment the rat was put into the shock side of the cage. A light went on, the floor slid away and the rat received a shock. Running around frantically to escape the unpleasant sensation, the rat, like Thorndike's cat, apparently jumped over the wall quite by accident. After a few trials, the rat not only learned to jump the wall to escape the shock but avoided the shock altogether by jumping the wall as soon as the light went on.

Then the shock apparatus was disconnected. But the rat never waited around long enough to discover that fact. If a person who knew nothing of the experiment walked into the lab and saw the rat jump the wall every time the light went on, he would conclude that he was looking at a crazy rat most illogically jumping a wall when a light went on.

The obvious inference is that many of the strange, illogical behaviors of people are the result of some kind of avoidance learning. To use a simple illustration (for which I am indebted to Dr. Willard Mainord of the University of Louisville), suppose a boy is taught by his father that it is a very bad thing to be a sissy, that he ought to stand on his own feet and be a man. Further, suppose that there is a large bully at the boy's school who regularly beats up the boy at school—definitely an unpleasant experience.

How is the smaller boy to avoid the unpleasantness, for he cannot go to his father, teacher or anyone else without appearing to be a sissy? One solution is for the boy to stop going to the playground at recess.

Suppose the bully seeks him out as he walks to and from school. Eventually, the boy is driven to playing hooky. Because he doesn't go to school, he gets into trouble with the principal and his parents. Asked where he was, he lies. An array of behavioral problems result from the boy's failure to attend school. A school psychologist is consulted. His home life is probed and there is talk of his Oedipal conflict.

This illustration is admittedly oversimplified, but it is possible to see how avoidance learning can lead to many untoward behaviors. It also shows how anyone not knowing the history of the avoidance learning would be hard pressed to explain the strange behavior.

If we return to the experiment of Mowrer and Miller, we can learn another thing about avoidance learning. The psychologists tried to "untrain" the rat not to jump over the wall and cause it to discover that the grid would no longer administer shocks. They found such retraining to be very difficult. But it can be done, as we shall see in the next chapter.

Another great contributor to studies of instrumental learning is *B. F. Skinner* of Harvard University. His work has had a profound effect on psychology and psychotherapy, for he has refined instrumental conditioning into *operant conditioning* by showing the rules of learning when an animal (including man) is operating on its environment.

Dr. Skinner's basic experiment was simplicity itself. He designed a box in which a pigeon could obtain a grain of corn by pecking a button. He also used a similar device in which a rat obtained food by pressing a lever. From what we have already learned, it is easy to understand that the pigeon would learn quickly to peck the button to obtain food. In learning theory terminology, the pigeon has received a *positive reinforcement*, a grain of corn, by learning to peck a certain spot. It is likewise understandable by now that the pigeon would unlearn his pecking procedure if pecking did not result in the reinforcement of corn. This process, you remember, was called *extinction*.

Skinner proposed to discover more. How would learning occur if the pigeon received corn only every fifth peck—or every tenth, or twentieth? And what would happen if the corn arrived randomly, that is, just now and then, without any regularity? Skinner put his pigeons to pecking away. As they did, Skinner maintained careful records of the number of pecks and the time elapsed for learning or unlearning. These statistics were reduced to graphs. In short, Skinner approached his studies with a great deal of scientific precision.

The results were a bombshell for psychology and an

instant controversy in psychotherapy. Reduced to simple terms. Skinner discovered that the pigeon would learn to peck very quickly if it received a reinforcement of corn. It also stopped pecking rather quickly when it did not get the corn. But if the pigeon got the corn only occasionally, it would continue to peck for a very long time.

Stated in broader terms, Skinner's discovery was that learning in animals (including man) is a product of reinforcement. If the learning results in positive reinforcement, the learning will take place quite rapidly and efficiently. If the learning does not result in positive reinforcement, the learning will be abandoned quickly. If the reinforcement occurs irregularly, the learning will take place more slowly, but it will be abandoned less easily.

These principles are easily illustrated. We used the example before, in referring to extinction, that if you were accustomed to being paid every Friday, you would stop working when the pay was not forthcoming. Now suppose you were paid irregularly. The boss gave you some money every so often, when he had it. In that event, you would probably continue to work for a very long time before you realized you were not going to be paid any more. In the other previous example, if there is a girl you find attractive and would like to date, you will stop asking her out if she always says no. But if she occasionally says yes, you will continue to ask her out over a long period of time.

The repercussions of this are in the category of shattering. Suppose there is a boy in your class who misbehaves as a means of gaining attention—that is, attention is his reinforcement. The teacher recognizes this and, using common sense, decides to ignore the boy. She is thus attempting extinction by denying the reinforcement. Under another learning principle, the immediate result is that the boy misbehaves more. It is as if he says, "This always worked in the past. I must not be doing as well or trying as hard." If the teacher continues to ignore the worsened behavior and no other kids in the class reinforce the boy through snickering or other forms of attention, according to learning theory extinction of the misbehavior will occur. All this is, of course, rather difficult to accomplish in a regular classroom.

Suppose a girl in this hypothetical class is a shoplifter. She regularly or frequently helps herself to items from the local stores. She is rather adept at this and is only occasionally caught. Say she succeeds five times for every failure. Under learning theory, she will continue to steal for a long time, barring other circumstances—of which more in a moment. If this theory is true, the repercussions in the field of crime and law enforcement will be large, to say the least.

Skinnerian principles are widely used in animal training. If you wish to train a chicken to play baseball, you can do so with a little patience. It is a process of step-by-step reinforcement. When the chicken goes up to home plate you give it some corn. After a few trials, it will always go to home plate for the corn. Then you withhold reinforcement until it runs to first base. The same process is repeated at second, third and back to home. If in the process you want to train it to swing an appropriately sized "bat" and hit a "ball," you could do that, too. Just observe the next animal act you see at the circus or on television. At some point the trainer will slip some food to the animal. It is his reinforcement.

People can also be trained by Skinnerian methods. A harmless example is the training a psychology professor received from his college class. The students got together and arbitrarily decided to train him to teach from the far lefthand corner of the room. Their reinforcement was to be attention. When he began his class, he was monumentally ignored. The students looked out the window, yawned and engaged in other acts of inattention. But when he made the slightest move to the left, he immediately gained the class' attention. They busily wrote in their notebooks and so on. Gradually, the professor was required to move ever farther to the left to gain attention. Soon he was delivering his lectures from the far left-hand corner of the room to his rapt students.

The startling fact about this incident is that the professor never knew why he had begun to lecture from that unusual position in the room. The training occurs even if the person knows nothing about it, and even if he has no desire for the learning.

Many, many similar experiments have been done. An amazing example is the work of Goldiamond and associates. They teach people to stammer without their being aware of how or why they suddenly lost their highly articulate speech. The subject is asked to read some material aloud while hooked up to a shock machine. Everytime he makes a slip of the tongue or mistake in reading, he receives a mild but unpleasant shock. The device is arranged so that after giving a shock, it shuts off for a given period of, say, ten seconds. One way, then, to keep from being shocked is to stammer more often than every ten seconds. Without any knowledge of what is happening to him or what he is supposed to do, the subject soon learns to stammer so as to keep the machine shut off. One subject reported, in a stammer of course, that the machine must be broken for he wasn't getting shocked.

Don't worry about the newfound stammerer. The process is then reversed and the subject is retrained back to normal speech.

There have been fascinating uses of such techniques in psychotherapy, which we will take up in the next chapter.

Thus far we have spoken of positive reinforcement. It is also possible to use *negative reinforcement*. Instead of a reward for an action, a punishment is inflicted. This also works. A person will stop doing something because it results in unpleasant or undesirable reactions. Skinnerian therapists have found punishment to be a more difficult and uncertain means of reinforcement than positive ones, although negative reinforcement has its uses.

Much interesting study has been made of the uses of punishment in learning theory. A psychologist named Solomon did an interesting experiment with dogs. He sat in his laboratory with a rolled-up newspaper. On one side of him was a bowl of conventional dog food. On the other was a container of boiled horsemeat, a delicacy for dogs. Working on the premise that it was wrong for the dogs to eat the horsemeat, he sought to teach the dogs this in two different ways, using negative reinforcement. Half the dogs were swatted with the rolled newspaper when they approached the horsemeat. The other half were permitted to take a mouthful of the meat before being swatted.

Then Solomon left the room with the dogs in a state of hunger. Eventually all the dogs nibbled the forbidden horsemeat. When Solomon next entered the laboratory, he was greeted by dogs displaying two types of reactions. The dogs he had punished before they tasted the horsemeat greeted him with wagging tails and affection. It was as if, having done the forbidden, they were totally unconcerned. The dogs which had been previously punished for having eaten the horsemeat skulked and cowered in the presence of Solomon. The implication of this experiment is that although a person will feel guilty for doing a forbidden act for which he has been previously punished, he will not feel guilty if punishment has kept him from a forbidden act which he later performs.

Such research has led to some "rules of punishment," some of which are in conflict with popular thinking. If unwanted behavior is to be eliminated, the punishment must be of sufficient intensity. The word *sufficient* leaves the punishment open to all gradations, but the point is that the proverbial slap on the hand for a serious offense is not effective. If a parent is going to spank a toddler for crossing the street unmindful of cars, then the spanking must be sufficiently hard to hurt. The shoplifter in the previous example must be punished—if punishment is to be used—sufficiently severely to offset the lure of her success. Either that or she must fail all the time.

With animals other than humans and with young children, the punishment must follow the unwanted behavior immediately. An example is the person who tries to teach his dog not to chase cars. The usual method is to call the dog and then punish him. But this will not work, for the action immediately preceding the punishment was calling the dog. The person is actually teaching the dog not to come when called. The best training is to have a helpful neighbor drive by while the dog's owner throws an ammonia solution on the animal as he chases the car. A few trials and the dog will learn.

Older children and adults have the capacity to have punishment deferred and still be effective. If the mother says "Wait till your father comes home!" and father does indeed punish the child later in the day, they may be correcting unwanted behavior. But there is reason to believe that, even in the case of adults, delay in punishment dilutes its effectiveness. One reason a criminal may not be reformed in prison is that the punishment takes so long and occurs (because of court trials and appeals) so long after the crime was committed. Besides, he was probably successful in crime several times for every failure.

Another rule: if a person is to receive the same punishment for the same misbehavior, the severity of the punishment must be greatly increased. If the toddler who was spanked for playing in the street does so a second time and is to be spanked again, then he must be spanked considerably harder. Such gradations are hard to judge.

If the misbehavior is a result of a previous punishment, the new form of punishment must be changed. Suppose a child steals and is spanked as punishment. If he then steals and lies about it and is again spanked, all he is being taught is to tell bigger and better lies. The lying is a result of the previous punishment. Some other form of punishment must now be used.

The final rule is that at the same time an undesirable behavior is being punished, a positive reinforcement should be given to achieve a desired behavior. A simple example might be the child who steals. It is stealing that is to be punished, not having money, which in itself is a desirable goal. At the same time a child is punished for stealing, he could be given an opportunity to earn some money.

These rules create some unavoidable difficulties when attempts are made to use negative reinforcement. It is quite possible, for example, to make a punishment into a reward. Suppose a child misbehaves. His mother inflicts some sort of mild punishment, such as a scolding; then a few minutes later—trying to return peace to the home or make up with him—she gives him a snack of cookies and milk. The latter acts as a positive reinforcement, teaching the child to endure the mild scolding to get the pleasant reward. The romantic institution of "kissing and making up" may be another example. Here again, the unpleasantness of the quarrel may actually be sought as a means of obtaining the rewards that follow.

This has been a necessarily brief presentation of some of the major areas of learning theory. We must now examine some of the ways this has been used by psychotherapists.

10

Therapy
Through Learning

Learning therapists have virtually no concern for motivation. They never ask why a person behaves in a certain way. Their concern is the behavior itself. They attempt to change rather specific behaviors. When constructive change has occurred, they consider the treatment successful. Few learning therapists work with a person in terms of his whole personality. They are little concerned with such matters as "life style." They are interested in specific "symptoms" which they can measure and change.

Learning theory has been applied to therapy for a long time. Mary Cover Jones's work with Peter and his fear of animals is an example. Another is the work done in the 1930s by O. Hobart Mowrer (whom we met before with the wall-jumping rat) and his wife, Molly. Mowrer sought to use learning theory to develop a cure for enuresis, which is persistent bed-wetting beyond the age when a person normally has control of his bladder. It is a fairly common complaint and grossly embarrassing to the child and his parents.

Freudian psychologists tend to treat the condition in Oedipal terms or as a symptom of insecurity. The child's home life is investigated to determine why he has conflict with his parents. The results of such methods have not been notably successful.

Ignoring insight, Mowrer hypothesized that the child simply does not get the message that he needs to urinate, or that he sleeps so soundly that he doesn't awaken to take appropriate action in the bathroom. He devised a pad for the child to sleep on, which turned on a light when it was touched by a drop of liquid. The light awakened the child and he went to the bathroom. Mowrer continued the treatment until the child had gone two straight weeks with a dry bed. He and his wife conducted the experiment with a significant number of children. Most were cured of bed-wetting after two weeks. A few relapsed and needed additional retraining. In some cases the treatment lasted nearly a year. But Mowrer was able to report 100 percent effectiveness with his method. Other therapists have tried the same method, reporting over 90 percent effectiveness.

Learning therapists like to talk about Mowrer's work with enuresis in two ways. First, despite its proven effectiveness, it is little used. Parents still take their bed-wetting youngsters to insight therapists who probe his psyche and seek reasons for his lack of bladder control, with results that are considerably less efficient. Second, Mowrer's work indicates the bed-wetting *causes* insecurity and emotional problems and is not a *result* of it. The child is embarrassed by his lack of bladder control. He is pressured by his parents. He feels inferior and insecure. All is a result of bed wetting. The insight therapists, finding insecurity, assume it is the cause and not the result.

One of the most celebrated and respected of the learning therapists is *Joseph Wolpe* of South Africa. His system, called *reciprocal inhibition*, is widely known and often reported. For more than a quarter century he has reported "cure" rates in excess of 90 percent. In psychotherapy this is phenomenal.

Do you remember Mowrer and Miller and their rat that jumped the wall as a product of avoidance learning? Mowrer found it extremely difficult to teach the rat to wait around long enough to learn that he no longer received a shock. Wolpe designed a different experiment with the same aim of reconditioning avoidance learning.

He put a cat in a cage that administered a painful shock. Although the cat jumped and howled and screamed, there was no way for it to avoid the shock. After a few trials, the cat exhibited similar behavior not only whenever it was put in the cage—even after no shock being administered—but also whenever it was placed near the cage and even when it was in the same room with the device that had inflicted the pain. Wolpe's problem then became similar to Mowrer's and Miller's, how to train that cat to enter the cage voluntarily and discover that it would not receive a shock.

Wolpe did this by constructing a series of cages and rooms progressively dissimilar from the original cage. Ultimately he constructed one so different from the original one that the cat would enter it to eat and perhaps to take a nap. Gradually, Wolpe put the cat in cages and rooms progressively more and more like the original one, in each instance feeding the cat, so that it discovered it had nothing to fear. At the end of this process—although there were some relapses—the cat was back in the original cage having lunch.

How might such an experiment be applied to humans? One of Wolpe's famous cases illustrates his technique. The patient, a bus driver, had an extreme fear of blood. If he came upon an accident in which a victim was bleeding, he was so upset and became so physically ill that he had to leave the scene. He had a blood phobia.

In a series of exhaustive interviews with the patient Wolpe determined that the patient feared only human blood, not animal blood. Then, Wolpe and the patient constructed a hierarchy of fears. The patient was most upset at a serious accident that left bleeding bodies lying around. He was less upset when a victim was walking around but bleeding from a cut. He was still less upset when he looked at a bleeding wound or at a bloodstained bandage. And he experienced the least fear when he knicked himself while shaving. When completed the hierarchy consisted of 15 progressively fear-producing situations involving blood, from a shaving knick to open carnage.

Wolpe next taught the patient how to relax. He used a technique in which the patient progressively tenses and then relaxes various muscles of the body until he achieves a state of relaxation. When the patient was totally relaxed, Wolpe began to describe the least fear-producing situation involving blood. When the patient felt any anxiety, he was to raise his finger. Wolpe then retreated from the situation in his description until the patient was again relaxed. Treatment involved a gradual progression through the fear-producing hierarchy until the patient experienced no fear while a scene of carnage was being described.

At the same time Wolpe gave the patient parallel assignments in accordance with the hierarchy, such as walking by a hospital, bandaging a cut finger, visiting an injured person, and viewing bandages. In a relatively short time the bus driver was so calm at the sight of blood that when he came upon an automobile accident he assisted in placing the victims in an ambulance.

Wolpe has applied the same technique for persons who fear heights, animals, enclosed places and many other special things. The technique is believed to be excellent for treatment of phobias but is considered less effective in treating other forms of behavior. However, Wolpe continues to expand his method.

Another approach to the same problem has been devised by *Thomas Stampfl*, a psychologist from Cleveland, Ohio. Stampfl reports a success ratio of well over 90 percent with his *implosive therapy*. Others who have used his method also find it successful.

Stampfl began with the same problem as Wolpe, the rats of Mowrer and Miller. How could they be made to wait around to discover that they would no longer be shocked? To create his strange-acting rats, Stampfl made a somewhat different box. His was in the shape of a long alley in which a light went on, then a buzzer sounded, after which half the floor slid away and the rat was shocked by a grid. The rat quickly learned to run, when the light went on, to the safe end of the box where it was not shocked. So intense was this avoidance learning, that the rat still ran to the opposite end of the box when the light went on after a thousand trials.

Stampfl attacked the reconditioning process boldly and simply. He tilted the box at such an angle that the rat could not physically run uphill to escape the grid. The light went on, the buzzer sounded, the floor moved

—and nothing happened. The rat learned that it got no shock. After a few trials, the box was returned to the level and the rat no longer engaged in his avoidance activities.

Applying this to human fears, Stampfl independently developed a technique of therapy that is both similar to and markedly different from Wolpe's. Stampfl also conducts interviews to learn the various gradations of a patient's phobia. Take, for example, the case of a person who fears heights and whose greatest fear is of standing atop the Empire State Building in a windstorm. Omitting any relaxation technique, Stamfl forces his patient to listen to the most frightening and vivid description of standing on a high building in a bad storm—tornado, perhaps. The patient feels terrible anxiety, yet there he is in the office, entirely unhurt. The experience is repeated until the patient no longer has any fear of the symbolic situation. The patient is also instructed to place himself in actual situations that formerly made him afraid.

Repeated studies by other psychologists indicate that the methods of Wolpe and Stampfl, while differing, are about equally effective. Both seem to be most effective in treating phobias, although Stampfl's technique has been used to treat stuttering also.

The Operant therapists (or "Skinnerians") who use the learning theories based on the work of B. F. Skinner have produced astounding results. They have a history of taking the most difficult, intractible cases, with whom all other methods of therapy have failed, and achieving significant improvements and cures.

The Skinnerians use reinforcement, usually positive but occasionally negative, to change specific behaviors.

There is reason to believe that the technique can be used to teach anyone to do anything, if the therapists have control over the reinforcements. One example occurred several years ago in Canada, when Skinnerian approaches were still in the experimental stage. The subject of the experiment was a fifty-four-year-old schizophrenic patient who had been hospitalized for twenty-three years. The woman's principal activity during those years had been to lie abed and smoke cigarettes. Careful observations were made of her activity. She spent sixty percent of her waking time in bed and about twenty percent sitting and walking. The rest of the time was used for meals, grooming and elimination.

To provide her with a novel type of behavior, it was decided to teach her to hold a broom while in an upright position. To accomplish this, the psychologists used cigarettes as a reinforcement. The only way the patient could obtain a cigarette was to stand and hold a broom. Cut off from cigarettes, she engaged in a variety of random behaviors, which eventually involved approaching a broom. At this point she received a cigarette. The cigarette was gradually withheld until she took hold of the broom. She quickly developed a new pattern of behavior in which she paced the floor holding a broom and smoking cigarettes. If anyone tried to take the broom away from her, she became angry and aggressive.

At this point, a psychiatrist of more Freudian persuasion was asked to observe the patient. Knowing nothing of the patient and her history, he wrote as follows:

> Her constant and compulsive pacing holding a broom in the manner she does could be seen as a ritualistic procedure, a magical action. When regression conquers the associative process, primitive and archaic forms of thinking control the

behavior. Symbolism is a predominant mode of expression of deep-seated unfulfilled desires and instinctual impulses. By magic, she controls others, cosmic powers are at her disposal and inanimate objects become living creatures.

Her broom could be then:

1. A child that gives her love and she gives in return her devotion:
2. A phallic symbol:
3. The sceptre of an omnipotent queen.

Her rhythmic and prearranged pacing in a certain space are not similar to the compulsions of a neurotic, but because this is a far more irrational, far more controlled behavior from a primitive thinking, this is a magical procedure in which the patient carries out her wishes, expressed in a way that is far beyond our solid, rational and conventional way of thinking and acting.

There was, of course, nothing irrational or magical in the woman's behavior. She was simply obtaining cigarettes.

A far more useful example of the Skinnerian techniques involves a young woman suffering from an acute case of *anexoria nervosa*. This is a condition in which the person refuses to eat. This patient had undergone a variety of therapeutic treatments, but to no avail. When she was near death from starvation, a team of operant therapists were given an opportunity to save her life.

They studied the woman's situation. She was housed in a sunny, pleasant hospital room. There were flowers, books, a phonograph and other appurtenances aimed at making her life as happy as possible. She received many visits from her family, friends and the hospital staff, all of whom exhorted her to eat.

Operant therapists frequently use food as a reinforcement. But this was impossible in this case. What reinforcement could be used to get the patient to eat? The Skinnerians decided to use a social reinforcement. The patient's family and the hospital staff objected, but, because the woman was so near to death, they agreed to the program that was set up.

The patient was moved into a bare, cell-like room devoid of any pleasantness or distractions. All other persons were forbidden to enter her room except the therapists. At mealtime, he would take her tray of food to her, remaining absolutely silent and oblivious to her existence. He would remain so until she took a bit of food. At this point he spoke to her. He would not speak again until she had taken a second bite, and a third, and so on. In this way the woman was gradually nursed back to health, although the ravages of starvation left her with serious health problems for a long time. Eventually she began a career working with mental patients.

In learning-theory terms, the therapists used speech or sociability as reinforcement to teach this person a new pattern of behavior involving eating and reacting with people.

Even more startling is the work of *Ivar Lovaas* and associates. They work with *autistic* children, long considered the most difficult form of functional psychosis to treat. The autistic child seems to be totally unresponsive to a social environment. He never learns to talk, or quits talking if he ever learned. He appears to have no feeling for people as people, but rather views them as objects. Severe cases are considered intractible, and it was a group of such children that Lovaas assembled. They were children with whom all methods of treatment had failed. All were considered hopeless cases.

It is not possible to describe Lovaas' methods in detail here, but he began his treatment with this attitude: if the autistic children were viewed behaviorially with no thought given to insight into their problems, the quality most observed was their complete lack of social skills. It was this he decided to teach. It is impossible to be a social animal without some form of speech, so it was this that he decided to try to teach first.

It was necessary in the beginning to teach the child to imitate. There were many exercises, but an example would be for the therapist to put a ball in a cup. The ball and cup were placed in front of the child. When he put the ball in the cup, the therapist said "good" and gave the child some food reinforcement. A fantastic number of trials were needed, but eventually the child regularly put the ball in the cup. The trials were continued until the child learned to imitate a variety of motor behaviors.

The same process was used to teach the patient to speak. The therapist made a sound. When the child made any sound in return, such as a grunt, he was reinforced with food. Gradually the contingency was changed. The child had to make a sound which more closely resembled that of the therapist. In time, the child learned to imitate a variety of words and phrases. The training continued until the child could identify a word with an object, such as "book" or "ball." The next step was for the child to respond through thought and not simply imitate. If, for example, the therapist said "Say 'ball'," the child would utter the word "ball" and not imitate.

Eventually Lavaas was able to drop the food reinforcement and use a word of praise for the same purpose. His formerly hopeless autistic children were brought to the level of the beginnings of communicative speech. He also trained them in affectionate behavior, so they were able to start to interact socially. Similar methods are now in use with autistic children in a number of institutions.

Operant therapy may well be, as some contend that it is, the most powerful tool for changing behavior that the world yet knows. But it has limitations. It is best used in an institutional setting, where the therapist has control over the patient and the reinforcements. It is being used with some out-patients in clinics, but in general it is less effective outside of institutions.

Operant therapy is also limited in its ability to cope with behaviors that are a product of interpersonal relationships. We all learn behaviors as a result of our dealings with parents, brothers and sisters, friends, teachers, employers, and many others. These are the biggest body of learned behaviors, and operant therapy is less successful in changing such behaviors. The reinforcements, which come from other people, cannot be controlled, certainly outside of an institution. But for changing specific behaviors of even the most difficult mental patients, operant therapy is highly effective.

The term *social learning therapy* has been applied to the efforts to change unwanted behaviors which result from interpersonal relationships. Social learning therapists are attempting to deal with the same unhappy, unproductive, self-defeating, rigid, socially inept, unloved and unloving people as the insight therapists. But rather than seeing the causes of such behavior rooted in Freudian, Neo-Freudian or some other event or condition involving insight, the social learning therapist thinks in learning-theory terms. He does not usually ask why a person does something, but what he is doing and how the behavior might be changed.

The social learning therapists share a kindredship with Wolpe, Stampfl, the Skinnerians and others and will use these techniques when they seem appropriate. But they are searching for methods to apply learning theory to social relationships.

How do we learn unwanted behavior from other people? There are myriad ways, the learning therapists believe, but consider these few examples: the child growing up in the urban ghetto learns perhaps hunger, privation, disrespect for schooling, stealing and lawbreaking, all from his family, friends and environment. A child of rich parents perhaps learns to be snobbish, spoiled and selfish, disinterested in other people. A successful thief perhaps learns to steal more skillfully and more often, or thinks that he ought to try to. A successful student or athlete learns that hard work and self-discipline lead to accolades and a sense of well-being, along with tangible rewards.

It is possible to be far more specific about how this learning is believed to occur. Dr. Mainord, referred to previously, presents a hypothetical case of the effects of learned behavior from social relationships. A happily married, successful and reasonably moral man begins a love affair with another woman. They meet secretly and the husband conceals the romance from his wife for some time. Then he is found out. He has told his wife he was working late at the office, but his wife wasn't to call there because the office didn't like wives to call. But an emergency occurs at home and she calls anyway, discovering that he is not in. When asked about it later, he lies, saying that he had to go out on business. He makes up a new excuse. It works for a while, but again he is caught in a lie. Soon, he is involved in a web of lies, deceit, secret meetings and phone calls. This not only is very demanding on him physically and mentally but also leaves him emotionally upset with both guilt and fear that he will be found out. His happy family life would be shattered by divorce or lack of trust.

Soon, his wife no longer believes his lies. Perhaps she has direct evidence of his unfaithfulness. They quarrel. He begins to blame her for his weariness and emotional upsets. He finds excuses for it, blaming the children, the need for money, the demands on his time. The lies and quarrels and emotional upheaval worsen. Meanwhile, the girl friend is demanding that he leave his wife and marry her. She wants more of his time and attention. His problems at home and with the lady friend take so much of his time and emotion that he begins to do poorly at his job. His employer also makes demands upon him, threatening to fire him or to take other punitive actions.

With continuation and acceleration of this pattern, the man begins to break down physically and emotionally. He begins to feel sorry for himself. His appearance becomes disheveled, he avoids work, cries a lot, and perhaps becomes so depressed as to withdraw from the world. He is a shell of his former self.

If this situation persists, some form of avoidance must be found. One way to solve all his problems is to become mentally ill. If he begins to have delusions, hallucinate, threaten suicide, become violent, or experience some other form of gross antisocial behavior, he will be committed to a mental hospital. When that happens, he will be "sick." The pressure from his wife, girl friend and employer will cease. One cannot be unkind to a person who is sick. He must be loved and taken care of.

Dr. Mainord and others believe that most, if not all, mental patients are a product of a similar process of learning involving social relationships. They believe the so-called "mental patient" is using his "illness" for a "payoff," that is, to get some gain from others or as a means of avoiding unwanted consequences. One method of treatment is to take the payoff out of the mental illness by making demands on the patient, requiring him to work, or in general stopping the gain he receives.

Dr. Mainord tells of one of his patients who had the delusion that his backbone had been replaced with manure. Whenever the slightest demand was made on him in the institution, he began delusioning about his backbone. The demands ceased. But, because he was harmless, he was permitted to return to his home on a weekend pass.

When the patient came to Mainord for a weekend pass, the doctor said, "We have been studying your case. We have concluded that your backbone really is filled with manure. Under this circumstance, we couldn't possibly allow you out of the hospital. We must look after you. In fact, you will have to remain in bed. We can't let a man in your condition wander around the institution." It was the last anyone heard of the delusion. Dr. Mainord calls it "the fastest orthopedic cure on record."

The leading social learning therapist is *Dr. O. Hobart Mowrer*, whom we have encountered a couple of times previously. Among social learning therapists, including even those who disagree with his theory and methods, he is believed to be the first man since Freud to offer a completely new explanation for mental disorders.

Mowrer believes mental disorders arise from three sources of discomfort—guilt, fear of exposure, and es-

trangement from the social community. He believes
guilt arises from a consciousness of misbehavior and a
conviction that it is necessary to try to maintain secrecy,
and that this in turn leads to social isolation. The symptoms of "mental illness," in Mowrer's opinion, either are
an effort to cope with guilt—the most important reason
—or are behaviors aimed at maintaining secrecy or
deception. In either case, the person reacts either by
anxiety or by withdrawal. Mowrer's theory contains one
other major point: that the therapist himself serves as a
model for the person he is trying to teach.

Mowrer believes the aim of therapy is to teach the
person to become an open, nondeceptive person. In
therapy, he normally begins with individual interviews
in which the person tells his story about what is trou-
bling him. Because of the influence of Freudian analysis,
the person's problems are usually stated in medical
terms. He rarely talks of his own misdeeds.

After listening quietly, Mowrer responds that in his
experience emotional disturbances are usually related to
misbehavior. At least that was the case with him. He
then tells his own story, about his battle to surmount
emotional imbalance resulting from misbehaviors in his
own lifetime. He states that his misbehaviors long led
him into intense guilt, pervasive deceptiveness and social
isolation, all of which culminated in recurrent bouts of
depression. He explains that he found his own salvation
in openly admitting his mistakes and imperfections, by
atoning in so far as possible for the wrongs he had committed, and by maintaining a life style of continuing
openness to others.

Typically, the patient responds to Mowrer's *modeling*
of his own history, by reporting whatever misbehavior
of his own has been bothering him. He and Mowrer

discuss together how these misdeeds and his feelings of guilt and need to hide them have led to his present difficulties. Typically, the patient then says he feels better for having revealed his trouble.

Mowrer then invites him to attend a group session with other people, none of whom he knows. Perhaps he would like to bring along his wife or other significant person in his life. At the group session, he hears a number of other strangers describe the mistakes of their past and how they had been led to a better life by being frank about their actions and feelings. The patient becomes involved in the process.

In subsequent therapy, the patient is led to confess his past errors to all the significant people in his life and, insofar as it is possible, to atone for these mistakes. This might involve so little as making an apology, repaying some stolen money, or simply admitting a past action. Experience has shown that in 90 percent of the cases others already knew of the actions the person was so desperately hiding.

Having reconciled himself to the community in which he lives, the patient is admonished to keep himself open to public scrutiny at all times. This will make it easier for him to avoid misbehavior. Since his obligations are known to others, he will receive approval for living up to them.

Such a method might be considered a form of insight therapy because it deals so much with material from the past, but it is not. It is an exercise in changing *social* behavior by offering the person *social* reinforcement through the approval of others.

Mowrer's therapy has the advantage of being rather rapid and of being simple so nonprofessionals can make use of it. He has a following among clergymen and others doing counseling.

Another widely known social learning therapist is *Dr. William Glasser* of Los Angeles, author of the widely read *Reality Therapy: A New Approach to Psychiatry.* Glasser is a psychiatrist and not broadly trained in learning theory. But through practical experience he developed a method which relies heavily on learning theory.

Glasser believes the essential problem in all people, from mental patients to the self-defeating and unhappy, is their failure to fulfill their basic needs and to face the reality of the world around them. He sees the basic need as being "to love and be loved . . . and to feel that we are worthwhile to ourselves and to others." Our failure to love and be loved and to be worthwhile to ourselves and to others, he believes, is rooted in misbehavior or, as he puts it, irresponsibility. When a person acts in a responsible manner towards himself and to others, he will fulfill his basic needs.

He defines responsibility as fulfilling ones needs "in a way that does not deprive others of the ability to fulfill their needs." A responsible person can give and receive love and he has feelings of self-worth and others share this view. Glasser believes most mental patients and others who visit psychiatric offices, prisons or other such institutions either never learned to be responsible or have lost the ability.

The concept of responsibility, as set forth by Glasser, is difficult to describe except in terms of behavior, although Glasser does not advocate specific behaviors. But he believes a person should act in such a way as to fulfill the above-named basic needs. The person who engages in criminal activity, fails to work, and belies the trust others have placed in him will hardly receive love from others or have a feeling of self-esteem. He must so alter his behavior as to earn love and self-respect.

In therapy, Glasser first tries to set up an *emotional involvement* with the patient. This is not Rogers' unconditional positive regard, but Glasser does try to indicate that he cares about the patient, is interested in him and wants to help him fulfill his needs. This may be the most difficult part of the therapy, for disturbed people either do not know how to become involved with another human being or are resistant to it.

During the involvement-seeking period, Glasser endeavors to show the person that he is strong, mature, and responsible, earning the patient's respect. Much of the therapy consists of simple talk about a wide range of subjects, in which the therapist maintains an attitude of both regard and responsibility. Glasser maintains that any subject may be talked about, but he tries to limit the discussion to matters in the present. He feels the past is of no interest. It is a matter to be forgotten, for the essence of responsibility is that the person not blame past mistakes or past actions of others. He stands on his own two feet and goes forward—from today.

Likewise, insight into causes of present difficulties is avoided. Glasser insists that all that matters is *what* is being done, not *why*. Together with the patient, he seeks to uncover the misbehaviors that are causing difficulties and to develop a plan to cope with the problem in the future, a plan leading to love and self-esteem.

He has been particularly effective in working with delinquents and has applied his methods to education.

Like Mowrer, Glasser is using social reinforcement to change behavior and is thus a social learning therapist. It would seem at first glance that Mowrer and Glasser have widely different systems, but they are more alike than different. They have only a difference in emphasis. Where Mowrer emphasizes confession and openness, Glasser emphasizes responsibility. But Mowrer, through openness, is teaching repsonsibility and Glasser is using openness to arrive at responsibility.

These two attributes, openness and responsibility, are at the heart of a wide variety of social learning therapies. Some therapists see social relationships as a *contract*. A husband agrees to certain behaviors in return for his wife's agreement to other behaviors, and vice versa. There is an unwritten contract betwen parents and children. At the minimum, parents agree to provide food, shelter, clothing, discipline and opportunity, while the child agrees to make it possible to provide those basics and to make use of them. There are similar contracts between employer and employee (often in writing), and between neighbors, friends, clergymen and parishioner, teacher and student.

Some therapists help patients by spelling out the terms of these contracts or helping the person to do so. In some cases the contracts are put into writing.

Social learning methods have been widely used by groups who did not realize that was what they were doing. The most celebrated is the technique of Alcoholics Anonymous. For more than a quarter-century, AA has used openness and responsibility to help men and women defeat their alcohol habit. A feature of AA meetings is confession by members who describe their past drinking habits. They relate how their lives were ruincd and how they found the courage to quit drinking. Members mutually help each other to remain nondrinkers and to develop means for leading mature, responsible lives. This is pure social reinforcement.

Social learning therapy is also used by Synanon and other groups aiding narcotics addicts. Confession in group sessions occurs, but primarily the emphasis is on responsibility. Upon entering Synanon, the addict is treated as a totally irresponsible child. He is permitted no privileges and can do almost nothing without permission. Meanwhile, he is given the hardest, most unpleasant tasks. He earns both privileges and easier tasks by demonstrating his responsibility. If he can perform the onerous tasks and stay out of trouble, obeying the rules, he will gradually progress toward greater responsibility and trust. This, again, is pure social learning therapy.

Many other applications have been made among delinquents, mental patients, gamblers and criminals.

11

A Critique and Overview

Learning therapists are a small but growing minority in the profession in the United States. A number of universities are beginning to offer training in learning therapy, but the educational norm is Freudian or some other form of insight therapy. For this reason most of the learning therapists are men and women trained in insight therapy who later adopted the learning model. Most of them became disenchanted with Freudian methods, largely because of what they believed were their ineffectiveness. They searched for improved methods, and for many the search led to learning therapy.

The various learning therapies are severly criticized by insight therapists, and the learning therapists mount a defense of their systems.

Learning therapists point out the lack of effectiveness of Freudian and other insight therapies as a justification for learning therapy. They believe that most of the insight therapies, being statistically no more effective than no therapy at all, are thereby bankrupt or nearly so. Learning therapists do not claim to have all the answers in treating the mentally disturbed. But they insist that the learning model offers more hope for the future.

As evidence of this they cite a great many statistics showing that 80 to 100 percent of their patients have been cured or greatly improved. They contend it is possible for them to determine what a "cure" is and to keep records of patients' progress, something rather difficult for most insight therapists.

Moreover, learning therapists believe they can approach therapy in a scientific manner. They measure behavior, set up a program to change it and then measure the frequency of the new behavior. They are less dependent upon the patient's statement that he feels better or is happier or has greater understanding of his difficulties. Learning therapists can more factually determine that the patient has lost his fear of heights or other phobia, has stopped drinking or being addicted, has discontinued his delinquent behavior, or has begun to work regularly. Learning therapists believe that with time and wider application of their principles, a greater number and a greater variety of people will be helped by their methods —in a word, that the future lies with them.

Insight therapists frequently criticize learning therapy in this manner: Agreed, it is possible to teach a person to change a specific behavior, but if that is done and no effort is made to alter the basic motivations that caused the unwanted behavior, then some new, perhaps worse behavior will occur. An alcoholic may stop drinking but then become self-destructive. A child may be trained not to wet the bed only to have his anxieties expressed in some other fashion.

Learning therapists reply that there is very little, if any, evidence to support this contention. On the contrary, there is great evidence that changing undesirable behaviors does not lead to other unwanted behaviors. Tens of thousands of alcoholics, addicts, delinquents and other malfunctioning people have been successfully aided by learning therapy. Such people may have more than one self-defeating behavior or they may later develop a new one, but that is not evidence that the second misbehavior was caused by altering the first one.

A more serious criticism of learning therapy is that it is too mechanical and perhaps even dangerous. Man is not a rat or a cat or dog. Man has a soul. He remembers, learns, thinks. He experiences emotions. He laughs and cries. It is terribly dehumanizing to eliminate most of what makes a man unique and "train" him as one would a cat or rat. Some attention must be paid to man's inner emotions and motivations. He is not a "thing" to be used.

The most emotionally inflamatory criticism made of learning therapy is that it is "brainwashing." The term came out of the Korean War in the 1950s. There had been examples previously, but when a small group of American prisoners refused to come home and chose to remain in Communist China, Americans felt the men had been brainwashed. The term came to mean that techniques had been used to break the will of prisoners and to alter their thinking and behavior. As commonly understood, brainwashing involved gross mistreatment of a person, followed by large numbers of propaganda sessions citing the virtues of Communism. When the prisoner began to show attitudes favorable to Communism, he received positive reinforcement in the form of better treatment.

There is evidence that such techniques, if skillfully applied, will work in at least some cases. Since learning therapies, particularly operant therapy, have similarities to brainwashing—even though they are used for a far more humane purpose—there is a tendency to fear that such methods might be abused.

Even if it is true that destructive or unwanted (from a particular point of view) behavior can be taught through learning theory, there is no reason to suppose that it will be. Indeed, no one charges that the nation's many learning therapists have engaged in any such practices. The complaint is solely that the methods are similar, whether the behavior taught is constructive or detrimental.

What can be said of psychotherapy in general. whether based on insight or learning?

We can begin by saying that it is a rather new art or science, call it what you will. Modern methods have been around for about three-quarters of a century. There has been considerable progress in both theory and methods, considering the fact that in working with the human mind, emotions and behavior, therapists are treading unknown ground.

But the progress has been hardly enough, considering the need of mankind for help with these problems. War, riots, crime, violence, bloodshed, addiction, drunkenness, and other grossly antisocial behaviors—be they called "mental illness" or "maladaptive behaviors," unproductiveness, folly, greed, disatisfactions or unhappiness—are surely plagues upon mankind. They are surely conditions that psychotherapy can help to improve.

It is not an undue criticism of psychotherapy to say that it has not been as effective in these matters as it might have been, because it has wasted so much of its energies in internal conflict. Society's problems are worsening. Repeated studies have indicated that in-

creased population, industrialization and urbanization—
worldwide phenomena all—tend to exacerbate tensions
and strife. Surely continuation of the infighting among
psychotherapists is a luxury the world cannot long
afford.

Psychotherapists of whatever persuasion need to find
a way to decide what the goals of their profession are.
They need to standardize both their training and the
terms for the conditions their trainees are seeking to
treat. There surely will be, and needs to be, disagreement about theories and methods of treatment, but just
as surely there needs to be an atmosphere of cooperation
with a common goal.

A rational mind studying all these theories and methods can only suspect that none of them offers the perfect
treatment. At best, some or all of them are effective some
of the time in certain cases, failing in others. With an
attitude of cooperation it might be possible to standardize those methods which seem to be effective with certain
types of cases and to launch systematic research projects
to determine the uses of both insight and learning methods. With cooperation, new methods of treatment based
on combinations of various methods might be developed.

This book has briefly described many—although
hardly all—of the promising approaches to psychotherapy. Their variety indicates that progress has been made
and offers hope for the future. Persistent defense of one
system, while denouncing all others, is not contributing
to the effectiveness of psychotherapy. An era of cooperation is certainly needed.

Selected Reading

The number of books on the subject of psychotherapy is nearly infinite. Here is a list of general books on the subject:

Alexander, Franz G. and Salesnick, Sheldon T.; *The History of Psychiatry*; Harper & Row, New York; 1966.

Bremmer, Charles; *An Elementary Textbook of Psychoanalysis*; Doubleday & Co., Garden City, N. Y.; 1957

Brown, J. A. C.; *Freud and the Post-Freudians*; Penquin Books, Baltimore, Md.; 1961

Capretta, Patrick J.; *A History of Psychology in Outline*; Dell Publishing Co., New York; 1967

Eysenck, H. J.; *Fact and Fiction in Psychology*; Penquin Books, Baltimore, Md.; 1965

Ford, Donald H. and Urban, Hugh B.;*Systems of Psychotherapy*; John Wiley & Son, N. Y.; 1963

Hall, Calvis S.; *A Primer of Freudian Psychology*; World Publishing Co., New York; 1954

Harriman, Philip L.; *An Outline of Modern Psychology*; Littlefield, Adams & Co., Totown, N. J.; 1963.

Harper, Robert A.; *Psychoanalysis and Psychotherapy;* Prentice-Hall, Inc., Englewood Cliffs, N. J.; 1959.

Hilgard, Ernest R. and Atkinson, Richard C.; *Introduction to Psychology;* Fourth Edition; Harcourt, Brace & World, New York; 1967.

Murphy, Gardner; *Psychological Thought from Pythagoras to Freud;* Harcourt, Brace & World, New York; 1968.

Rogow, Arnold A.; *The Psychiatrists;* G. P. Putnam's Sons, New York; 1970.

Sargent, S. Stansfeld and Stafford, Kenneth R.; *Basic Teachings of the Great Psychologists;* Doubleday & Co., Garden City, N. Y.; 1965.

Small, Leonard; *The Briefer Psychotherapies;* Brunner/Mazel, New York; 1971.

Index